COUP D'ETAT ILLUSTRATED
VOLUME 001

Each generation must out of relative obscurity discover its mission, fulfill it, or betray it.
-Frantz Fanon,
The Wretched of the Earth

George "Squeeze" Morillo
Ricky Mujica

CONTENTS

OLD SCHOOL, TRUE SCHOOL
A LOOK BACK AT EARLY HIP-HOP PARTY FLYERS & FASHION

NEWS CLIPS BULLETIN BOARD
NEWSPAPER CLIPPINGS POSTED BY OUR READERS

THE UNDERWORLD
THE INCREDIBLE WORK OF OIL PAINTING MASTER **MAX GINSBURG**

MUG SHOTS
CELEBRITY PHOTO PAGES

FILM
JUSTIFIABLE HOMICIDE

BOOK
THE BANDANA REPUBLIC

ALBUM REVIEW
COMMON AND MARY MARY

O.G. FILES
INTERVIEW WITH OUTLAW LEGEND **ROBERT "CHINO" PEREZ**

INTERNATIONAL PHOTO PAGES
THE BEAUTIFUL COUNTRY & PEOPLE OF **BRAZIL**

FEATURES

HIP HOP REVOLUTIONARIES
CHE IN BLING?   BY EURAIH X. BENNETT

ICED OUT, ASSED OUT
HOW THE BLING-BLING MINDSET IS DESTROYING AFRICA   BY EURAIH X. BENNETT

GRAFFITI HALL OF FAME
AN NYC URBAN PHENOMENON SINCE 1981   BY GEORGE **"SQUEEZE"** MORILLO

NATIONAL CONFERENCE OF BLACK MAYORS
DOIN BIG THANGS   BY AVIS SKINNER

GLORY OF MY DEMISE
AUTHOR **KWAME TEAGUE** SPEAKS ABOUT HIS BOOK *THE ADVENTURES OF GHETTO SAM/GLORY OF MY DEMISE* AND HIS ROLE IN WRITING THE HOT-SELLING BOOK *DUTCH* WHILE SERVING DOUBLE LIFE SENTENCES IN A U.S. PRISON.   BY: ALEX MORFOGEN

THE DISCO FEVER
INTERVIEW WITH **SAL ABATIELLO** THE FOUNDER OF THE **DISCO FEVER** BACK IN THE **70S**   BY IVETTE **"THE DIVA"** VALENTIN

Editorial

Publisher/ Editor-in-Chief
George "Squeeze" Morillo

Deputy Editor
Ricky Mujica

Chief Financial Officer/Business Development
Euriah X. Bennett

Art Director/ Illustrator
Ricky Mujica

Director of Advertising/ Sales
Warren Davis

Print Production Manager
Jo-Ana Moreno

Creative Consultants
Wayne Robinson of SHIMMER Concepts Media, Inc.
PFI Marketing

Editorial Assistants
Naimah Holmes, Maria Scarfone

Distribution
ARAWAK Multi-Media

Legal Adviser/ General Counsel
Marisa Benton

Contributing Writers
Alex Morfogen, Ivette "The Diva" Valentin, Avis Skinner, Dana Holmes, Kwame Teague, Michelle Henriquez, Euriah X. Bennett, & Seph "Soul Man" Ferranti

Contributing Photographers
Suemyra, M1, DJ Oreon, Avis Skinner, George "Squeeze" Morillo

Coup D'Etat Illustrated is published bi-monthly by ARAWAK MULTI-MEDIA, LLC out of New York, New York. Copyright 2005 ARAWAK MULTI-MEDIA, LLC. "Coup D'Etat Illustrated" is a trademark of ARAWAK MULTI-MEDIA, LLC. All artwork is solely owned by Rick Mujica for Arawak Multi-Media, LLC. And cannot be used without written permission. All rights reserved. Reproduction in whole or in part without written permission is strictly prohibited.

Subscriptions request: Park West Finance Station, P.O. Box 20069 New York, NY 10025
Advertisers and Retailers please contact: coupdetatmag@aol.com or myspace.com/coupmagazine
Please visit our site at: www.coupdetatillustrated.com

Coup D'Etat Illustrated

• **Coup D'Etat**: a sudden decisive exercise of force in politics; esp.: the violent overthrow or alteration of an existing government by a small group.

• **Illustrated**: to make clear by giving or by serving as an example: to provide with visual features intended to explain or decorate; to show clearly.

Editor's Page
Until Makaveli's Return, All Eyes On Us

Coup D'Etat Illustrated is a publication that covers ~~~~~~~~~~~~~~~~ Hip Hop life style, ~~~~~~~~~~ Coup D'Etat ~~~~~~~~~~~~~~~~~~~~~~~~~~~~~~ FlashNewsMag.com ~~~~~~ This ~~~~~~ Coup D'Etat Illustrated with its unique ~~~~~~~~~~~~~ , and ~~~~~~~~~~~~~~~~~~~~~~~~~~~~~~~~~~~~~~ is like "The New Yorker", "Life", and "Time" magazine, making this an ~~~~~~ media ~~~~~~ quality of a printed publication. We believe that graphics are a vital part of mass communication ~~~~~~

Coup D'Etat Illustrated will address real issues concerning ~~~~~~~~~~~~ unities here ~~~~~~~~~~~~~~~~~~~~~~~~~~~~~~~~ community, ~~ of the political rap group, dead prez. Coup D'Et ~~~~~~ politics, ~~~~~~~~~~~~~~

I would like to thank everybody that made this thought a reality. I leave you with this quote from ~~~~~~~~~~~~~~~~~~~~~~~~~~~

If I Should Go, Follow Me.
If I Should Hesitate, Push Me.
If I Should Stop, Kill Me.

—George "Squeeze" Morillo

Old School,
-1978 Hip Hop Flyer-

True School
Hip Hop's Underground Fashion
New York City 1970's

INFLAMMATORY BREAST CANCER

Michelle (fourth from left) with friends at the 2006 Making Strides Against Breast Cancer walk in NYC

Just about every year I participate in the Making Strides Against Breast Cancer walk to make a difference in the fight against breast cancer. Often I am questioned as to why I would donate time, money and effort to find a cure for a disease that I don't have. My response to them has always been how could I not? Breast cancer is truly an epidemic among women and men. The truth is, breast cancer has affected and can potentially affect my life tremendously. I've watched family, neighbors, co-workers and close friends dealing with this everyday struggle and I'd be so out-of-touch with reality if I said that their struggles haven't affected me.

Many people don't realize that every two minutes a woman is diagnosed with breast cancer or that a girl's early onset of menses (her period) or a woman experiencing late menopause cause an increased risk of developing breast cancer. Risks also increase from diets high in saturated fat and even moderate obesity (two things Americans can't stay away from). One woman in eight who lives to age 85 either has or will develop breast cancer in her lifetime. A common misconception is that breast cancer is exclusively a disease of women. It is not. My friend's husband is a breast cancer survivor. In fact, 1,600 men will be diagnosed with breast cancer and 400 will die this year.

When breast cancer is found early, the five-year survival rate is 96%. Mammograms are among the best early detection methods, yet 13 million U.S. women 40 years of age or older have never had a mammogram. Mammography is a low-dose X-ray examination that can detect breast cancer up to two years before it is large enough to be felt. This is why I donate time, money and effort to this disease. People must know how this can affect them & what they can do to fight back. I feel that my participation is helping to spread the word to countless number of people (telling/emailing/posting to 5 friends & asking them to tell/email/post to 5 friends on my behalf). Over 2 million breast cancer survivors are alive in America today and I'd like to believe that I helped make that possible.

If you would like to participate in the Making Strides Against Breast Cancer walk, find other ways to support this event, or learn more about the American Cancer Society's mission, I encourage you to visit the American Cancer Society's Making Strides Against Breast Cancer web site at www.cancer.org/stridesonline.

Michelle C. Henriquez
Shearman & Sterling LLP
michelle.henriquez@shearman.com

HIP HOP: GLOBALIZED OR GLOBAL FORCE

Hip Hop has become globalized, but is has no global force, no global voice. This is not to be confused with its economic global impact, because the Hip Hop market doesn't necessary represent the culture itself. (And in many ways, contradicts it.) The energy of Hip Hop is spreading exponentially, but its weakness is inherent in its strength….
It's fluidity.
Just as water seeks its own level, individual creativity does the same, but like scattered rain showers or occasional monsoon, it batters weakly against the concrete forms of global imperialism, leaving only mired puddles at its base. We need a global typhoon, a tsunami that builds as it destroys. Destroys the racial complexities (without destroying identity), and destroys the political chasms while simultaneously building the global network paramount to our collective future of enlightenment and empowerment.
We need a global Hip Hop Nation.
Until now, the Hip Hop Nation has been more abstract than concrete, more visceral than pragmatic, but we need to establish it, we must establish it; because all over the world we are dying. More and more, in Nation after Nation (so-called advanced, developing or Third World), the youth are becoming increasingly disenfranchised, having a diminishing stake in the societies in which they dwell. The results are destructive pathologies of self destruction fueled by disregard and out-right abandonment of the governing powers.
What would be the nature of such an alliance? That isn't for one man to determine. First of all, we must agree that such an alliance is needed before we define its structure. But it should address the gamut, from economics to politics, in terms cultural as well as ideological. It should have a vision, but one grounded in realistic and feasible objectives, and not utopia delusions of grandeur. It should combine the spirit of Hip Hop's creative energy, embodied in Hip Hop's dynamics. In short, it should be!
The need is self evident, as world governments become more concerned with their own prosperity, leaving the masses to fend for themselves. And as human life gets cheaper, it is clear that the future is in our hands. If we fail to act, then the blame is our own, therefore the consequences, self inflicted.
Like the great Rakim once said, "it aint where your from it's where you at," so yo …Where you at?!!

Kwame Teague
Author of
"The Adventures of Ghetto Sam" And the "Dutch" Series

HIP-HOP REVOLUTIONARIES
CHE IN BLING?

By Euriah X. Bennett

Chuck D • Paris • Tupac • Stick Man • M1

"The revolution will not be televised."
- Gil Scott-Heron

And it won't be played on the radio either. Artists with a revolutionary commentary on current social economic affairs will almost certainly not hear their music on the local radio stations. You're not going to hear the rock group "Rage Against the Machine" or folk artist Ani de Franco on the radio. You're not even going to hear what Bob Marley REALLY had to say. Furthermore, revolutionary hip-hop artists, like Paris and dead prez, are not played on radio stations that would rather play Jay-Z's "Change Clothes" or the Terror Squad's "Lean Back." Curiously, Jay-Z claims to be, "Che in bling," referring to the Argentinean revolutionary leader who helped to liberate Cuba from American backed dictatorial subjugation. He went on to fight and die for revolution against colonialism all over the world. I realize that Che Guevara can't answer for himself, but I find it hard to imagine Che, who fought the CIA and Belgian soldiers in the Congo and was brutally hunted down by American mercenaries and killed in Bolivia, being reincarnated as Jay-Z in bling. Which begs the question, "Who are the revolutionaries of the hip-hop generation?" Who bears the legacy of musical inspiration and social commentary for the under 40 crowd? Which artists have been consistent in their delivery of socially poignant analyses, delivering flows that Che would have nodded his head to?

Black and Latino revolutionaries of the '60s and '70s liberation movement desired radical social change that would produce a fair and just society for all people. They were involved with changing political and economic conditions to ensure the well-being of the have nots. Recognizing that worldwide poverty existed alongside opulent wealth, wars of greed, and intense racism, Malcolm X advocated change to an inhumane system, "by any means necessary." He was part of long tradition of revolutionaries for social justice, including Denmark Vesey and John Brown, who led slave revolts, and the Black Panther Party with their survival programs to Patrice Lumumba, former Prime Minister of the Congo.

The spoken word of Gil Scott-Heron and the Last Poets arguably created the anthem for the Black liberation movement of the '60s and '70s. Mr. Scott-Heron's truthful, hard-hitting "raps", such as "The Revolution Will Not Be Televised" attacked the status quo, called the oppressor by name and provided uplifting words for those struggling in urban ghettoes. He and other poets/rappers of his time were predecessors to the rap music genre of today. In 1994, Mr. Scott-Heron made a song directed to "young rappers", as he referred to them, "Message to the Messengers." As the title suggests, he makes the link from his revolutionary rants of decades ago to the rapping of today. He encourages the young rappers and anyone of the hip-hop generation to build on a sense of community, develop their political awareness and to respect each other.

A generation passed before artists would walk the path that Mr. Scott-Heron walked before them. Oppressive social economic conditions that shaped gospel, the blues and the spoken word of Gill Scott-Heron and the Last Poets would ultimately be expressed through hip-hop music. Just as the Black and Latino artists who comprised the original members of the Last Poets represented the disenfranchisement of Black and Latino urban communities during the '60s and '70s, hip-hop developed from the oppressive conditions experienced by Black and Latino youth in later years. While early raps were fun and kept the party going, some raps had a degree of social commentary. These raps included "The Message" and "New York, New York" by Grand Master Flash and the Furious Five, "Hard Times" by Run D.M.C. and "The Breaks" by Curtis Blow. Since then, rappers like Tupac, the Coup, KRS 1, Paris, Mos Def and Chuck D have all continued the legacy.

2pacalypse Now

Tupac emerged as the "rebel of the underground" wearing a dashiki in a digital underground video. Both of his parents were members of the Black Panther Party. His mother, Afeni Shakur, was a leader in the NY Chapter of the Black Panther Party, holding the chapter's position of Minister of Defense. Like Malcolm, Tupac's early life was laced with seediness. Also, like Malcolm, he was cut down before he could reach his full potential.

Tupac talked of running for national office, of being the representative of the urban community and of radical social change. Some found his lyrics and actions controversial and contradictory. To some, including ex-Republican Senator Bob Dole and ex-Vice President Dan Quayle, Tupac's lyrics were sexist and celebrated gang life. To many others, his lyrics were uplifting and a reflection of inner-city struggles. While his use of the terms "bitches" and "ho's" to describe women were regrettable, the lyrics to songs such as Brenda's "Got a Baby" and "Keep Your Head Up" were anti-abuse and empowering. Tupac was able to channel the thoughts, dreams and experiences of disenfranchised young Blacks and Latinos through his music. Embracing "THUG life!" throughout many of his songs, his lyrics had undertones of retribution. Thug was an acronym for "The Hate U Gave". While Tupac's "gansta" behavior was much publicized, no event better illustrated the degree to which he personified his revolutionary lineage than his confrontation with two disorderly police officers in Atlanta in 1993. While riding in a car with an entourage in Atlanta, Tupac became enraged after noticing two men harassing a motorist.

Tupac confronted the men who identified themselves as police officers while wielding their guns and threatening Tupac with deadly force. This in no way gave Tupac pause. He pulled his own gun and shot the officers before they could do harm to him or anyone else. Tupac was initially charged, however the charges were dropped once the facts emerged. The policemen, had been drinking and had initiated the incident. In addition, the prosecution's own witness testified that the gun one of the officers threatened Tupac with had been seized in a drug bust and later stolen from an evidence locker. The real hero, protecting and serving the well-being of a victimized citizen, was Tupac. The shooting in Atlanta made him a hero to his community and a monster to police and conservatives. The shooting of the cops in Atlanta gave weight to Tupac's seditious rhetoric.

Bush Killer

West Coast rapper Paris defines himself as the Black Panther of hip-hop unquestionably aligning himself with the most militant revolutionary organization in modern American history. His lyrics support this contention. On his first album, he recites the Black Panther Party's original 10-point program, the cornerstone of Black Panther Party dogma; introduces the listener to important revolutionary names and personalities, and dramatizes militant actions as if he were riding shotgun with Huey Newton himself. His early raps metaphorically mention key names of the Black Panther Party, including Eldridge Cleaver along with Huey. Each of his four albums never strayed from the basic doctrine of the Black Panther Party. One could get a 1960s Black Power history lesson from listening to Paris.

The Black Panther Party captured the imagination of their generation. They often used controversial images to provoke critical thinking and inspire revolutionary action. The artwork of Emory Douglas, Minister of Culture, shocked and awed. He was the primary illustrator for the Black Panther Party newspaper. Similarly, Paris uses shocking images and statements to get his points across. His most recent album is titled *Sonic Jihad* (Jihad is an Islamic term meaning a crusade for a principle or belief) alluding to the current hysteria regarding Islamic references. In addition, the cover of the album shows an airliner flying directly at the White House, completing the unfinished business of 9/11 while hinting at the Bush Administration's complicity in the loss of innocent lives.

A revolutionary typically finds many aspects of the status quo systematically oppressive. News and information that challenge the establishment is often suppressed until a critical mass of support develops for certain issues or until the establishment's policies crumble under the weight of its own lies, deceptions and misappropriations. Paris was critical of the events surrounding 9/11 and the United States, response long before high-profile government officials and other individuals took up the cause.

Books by former Treasury Secretary Paul O'Neil as well as reporter Bob Woodward dismantle the Bush administration's hawkish orchestrations before 9/11 and are very popular with the mainstream. However, Paris' own analyses and conclusions regarding the wars in Iraq and Afghanistan foreshadowed the assertions made in those books. His *Web site*, guerillafunk.com, contains news and information that is unavailable in mainstream media. The site offers a video titled *Aftermath: Unanswered Questions* that investigates the conspiratorial events surrounding 9/11 nearly two years before Michael Moore's popular 9/11 analysis, *Fahrenheit 911*. While Paris's video came first, both productions suggest that Bush's complicity in the 9/11 attacks was inherent to garnering support for further military domination of the Middle East.

Messenger to the Messengers

In 1994, Gil Scott-Heron released his album *Spirits,* which included the pivotal spoken word titled "Message to the Messengers". In the lyrics, Mr. Scott-Heron encourages rappers to use their talents and platform to inform and uplift their community as he and others did in their time. He also tells rappers to take responsibility for misogynistic, self-hating and shameful lyrics that use unnecessary invectives that betray a lack of creativity and ignorance. By the time "Message to the Messengers" was released, Chuck D and Public Enemy had already fulfilled Mr. Scott-Heron's call for socially conscious rap. While Public Enemy released their first album in 1986, their influence would last for many years to come. On Public Enemy's second album, *It Takes a Nation of Millions to Hold Us Back*, Chuck D rapped about the evils of capitalism, a prison uprising and Black Nationalism. As the leader of Public Enemy, Chuck D waxed politically and poetically over samples, sirens, squeals and squawks, creating a sound that was radical, even for hip-hop. With little airplay or prime-time coverage, Public Enemy became one of the most notorious rap groups of all time.

While interest in Public Enemy music has waned, Chuck D has become a noted critic of the materialistic mentality of most mainstream hip-hop from a corporate perspective as well as an artist's perspective. In an interview with Jason Gross, Chuck D says, "Artists don't sell records, record companies sell records. Sales departments sell records. Artists should have an awareness of all the areas surrounding them. The artist should also understand that it's art first and everything else after that. If they really want to get into the selling of their own records, they should become their own record company and see how the sales department works. Don't just walk by floor number six like 'I don't need to know what the fuck is going on there.' Artists need to know the whole fucking game. That's why you see in Black music, you have executives who go to a point, become a dinosaur and then they don't go any further. They come up through marketing and promotion and they don't really know the other departments. Promotions are maybe a fifth of the major part of what makes the record company tick. People like Donnie Imus are well versed in maybe six or seven different areas. That's the training ground that Black executives haven't been given."

Revolutionaries often reach the conclusion that their prosperity rests outside of the current social economic system. Some, like Black Panther and Black Liberation Army member Assata Shakur, were forced into exile to evade persecution. Even Eartha Kitt voluntarily went to France to continue her singing and acting career after being marginalized for speaking out about the Vietnam War. Others remain but find ways to support themselves outside of the system. Tupac expressed this notion of seeking prosperity outside of the prevailing system by naming his supporting crew "Outlawz." It is rumored that before he died, he was looking for a way to cut his ties to Death Row Records and provide himself with a level of creative and financial autonomy. Both Chuck D and Paris find ways to distribute their music outside of the corporate infrastructure by using the Internet and grassroots support.

Chuck D has provided leadership in the rap game by being emphatically critical of the use of the N-word in rap lyrics. He is part of a documentary aired on VH-1 in July 2004 regarding the N-word. The documentary attributes the introduction of the N-word to mainstream society to Richard Pryor. Correspondingly, rap lyrics have given the word its worldwide reach. Chuck D's involvement in the documentary and his insightful comments support the fact that the word continues to be derogatory no matter how widely it is used. It is work such as this that enables Chuck D to give direction and enlightenment to the hip-hop masses. Ironically, Richard Pryor vowed to never use the word again after seeing so many people of his heritage during a visit to Africa.

Here is a hip-hop activist who has endured what most hip-hop artists are going through or hope to experience. Chuck D sets examples for ways to create self-sufficiency in the rap game based on his hands-on experience. He has explored distributing Public Enemy music through the Internet instead of through corporate distribution channels. As his quote suggests, he values understanding all levels of the record industry to minimize exploitation of the artist by corporations.

The late '80s to the early '90s is called the golden age of hip-hop and Chuck D and Public Enemy epitomized that era. At the time rap groups and rappers, like X-Clan, Queen Latifah, Brand Nubian, Ras Kass and Poor Righteous Teachers rapped about the plight of the urban community and Afro-centrism. Tupac and Paris attained their greatest success during that period. It's difficult to find rappers on the music scene today that are as consistently political as Chuck D and others from those years.

"dead prez" holds the mantle for delivering to the masses this era's conscious rap. Emerging underground rapper MF Grimm, AKA Jet Jaguar, fits the mold set by Tupac and Chuck D. Nas is promising on a number of raps including "If I Ruled the World" and "One Mic," however, he does not match the consistent example of the rap consciousness of Chuck D or the anti-establishment appeal of Tupac. Sista Solja, like Chuck D, has found avenues other than rap to provide social and economic comments. Known for her radical lyrics and activism, her book, *The Coldest Winter Ever*, tells the story of a young girl named Winter who comes of age in a drug infested world. The book creatively explores dismal values driven by poverty and racism and positive values like self-love and community empowerment. Talib Kweli can always be counted on to be a backpacker. Jadakiss raps on Why, "Why did Bush have to knock down the towers?" Like Paris, he accuses the Bush Administration of complicity in the destruction of the World Trade Center towers. In fact, Jadakiss's entire rap is a collection of one-liners on dire social and economic conditions particular to the Black and Latino community.

Hip-hop is arguably the most global music form in the history of civilization. Hip-hop can be heard at all ends of the earth: from Brazil, to South Africa to Germany to Japan. It has reached the point of ubiquity. It bridges cultures. Consequently, elements of it can be a force of social change and other elements can remain a tool of moneymaking conglomerates. The Revolution Will Not Be Televised", but hip-hop will make it heard all over the world.

CLIPS

NEWSDIGEST

Posada Carriles (AP)

U.S. seizes Cuban accused in bombing

MIAMI Under growing international pressure, U.S. authorities yesterday seized a Cuban exile accused by Fidel Castro's government of masterminding a 1976 airliner bombing that killed 73 people. Luis Posada Carriles, a 77-year-old former CIA operative and Venezuelan security official, had been seeking asylum in the U.S.

■ Russia to U.S.: Sign nonagression deal

Russia wants to negotiate a deal with the United States saying their militaries will not target each other, as a way to assuage concerns over U.S. plans to deploy missile defense sites in central Europe, a senior Russian diplomat said yesterday. (AP)

Mayor-elect killed self

WESTLAKE, La. — The first black mayor-elect in a largely white Louisiana town committed suicide days before he was to take office, the coroner said yesterday.

The body of Gerald (Wash) Washington, 57, was found Saturday night in the parking lot of a former high school with a pistol nearby. The mayor-elect's family did not accept the coroner's ruling and has asked for a state police investigation.

News Wire Services

■ Judge calls for reformed drug laws

A federal judge who once advocated harsher penalties for crack cocaine crimes said yesterday the policy had gone too far and was undermining faith in the judicial system. The current law includes what critics have called the 100-to-1 disparity: Trafficking in 5 grams of crack cocaine carries a mandatory five-year prison sentence, but it takes 500 grams of cocaine powder to receive the same sentence.

Somalia's government wants to go home

NAIROBI Somalia's parliament in exile yesterday approved the deployment of Ugandan and Sudanese peacekeepers to the troubled Horn of Africa nation, a senior government official said. The vote paves the way for troops to help the government to return from Nairobi, where it has been based because of unsafe conditions in Somalia. (AP)

Mex prez sorry for slur

MEXICO CITY — Mexican President Vicente Fox is apologizing — sort of — after whipping up a storm of criticism by saying illegal immigrants do work in the U.S. "that not even blacks want to do."

In a statement released yesterday, his office said Fox "conveys his utmost respect to all minorities regardless of their racial, ethnic or religious background, and thus, regrets and expresses his disagreement with the interpretations that described [his] statements as racist."

Fox made the inflammatory comparison after Congress passed immigration measures that made it tougher for illegal immigrants to get driver's licenses and authorized the extension of a fence between California and Mexico.

"The purpose of his comments was solely to stress the current importance of Mexican workers in the development and progress of U.S. society," Fox's statement said.

But commentators in his own country slammed him for the remarks and the Rev. Jesse Jackson said they had ominous racial overtones."

News Wire Services

Light shines on 'blood diamonds'

By Jennifer Redfearn
Special to amNewYork

The movie "Blood Diamond" brought attention to the issue of gems funding atrocities.

Diamonds are no longer every girl's best friend, but they are a complicated issue. The recent Hollywood blockbuster "Blood Diamond" made millions of people aware that these symbols of everlasting love also help fuel brutal wars and human-rights abuses.

Yet an absolute ban on the gems isn't the answer, according to Martin Rapaport, publisher of the Rapaport Diamond Report. He said that any dip in sales would harm the thousands of Africans who depend on the legal trade.

In addition to funding conflicts in Angola and the Democratic Republic of the Congo, the sale of diamonds sustained the recent 10-year civil war in Sierra Leone. During the war, the rebels hacked off their opponent's limbs and forced thousands of children to become soldiers.

In response to these human rights abuses and pressure from the nonprofit organization Global Witness, the U.N. backed a 2003 certification process that tracks the origin of diamonds so only stones from conflict-free zones enter the market.

Rapaport said he'd like to see a fair-trade system similar to the one in place for coffee, which would assure that those who mine the diamonds are treated and compensated fairly.

"You give a girl a fair-trade diamond, she's going to love you more because you're also altruistic," he said.

Groups sue FBI to release records on political activists

ACLU's Ann Beeson (Getty)

Five civil rights, animal rights and environmental groups are joining together to sue the FBI to release records about monitoring of anti-war and other political activities by federal agents assigned to counterterrorism duties.

The American Civil Liberties Union said the decision to file a lawsuit today in U.S. District Court in Washington came after the FBI ignored Freedom of Information Act requests for the documents.

"We think that if they have some reason to hide from the public the files they have on political and religious groups, we want to know right now what it is," said Ann Beeson, the ACLU's associate legal director. (AP)

■ HEALTH IN BRIEF

WHO, Gates give $50M to poor countries to improve their health information systems

The U.N. health agency and the Bill & Melinda Gates Foundation said yesterday they would team up to improve medical information systems for poor countries to help their fight against deadly diseases such as AIDS, tuberculosis and malaria. The Gates Foundation is pledging $50 million to the program — dubbed the Health Metric Network — which the World Health Organization's chief said was essential for poor countries if their health protection was to catch up with that of rich countries. (AP)

Bizarre photo

I'm writing to inform you that the photo of Benedict XVI in Friday's international section makes the pope appear to have horns. This is, of course, an illusion caused by a shirt collar of the man standing behind the pontiff. It is amusing, though it may offend some Catholics who will take this simple coincidence to mean that your newspaper is trying to vilify the new pope.

J.M. Grebski, Brooklyn

Cheap shot

I'm constantly amazed at the new ways the press finds to either attack or malign those they disagree with about social issues. That was a nice picture of the pope you printed on Friday which used the white collar of the man standing behind him to make it look like he has horns on his head.

It is way too obvious to be overlooked. Your less-than-subtle insult has been noted.

Janica Gill, Floral Park

The editors of amNewYork didn't notice the bizarre optical illusion in this AP photo of Pope Benedict XVI, which ran in Friday's issue. We apologize if the photo offended any readers.

Actress: 9/11 our fault

BY MAGGIE HABERMAN
DAILY NEWS STAFF WRITER

ACTRESS Maggie Gyllenhaal, star of a new flick about the aftermath of 9/11, believes the United States "is responsible in some way" for the devastating terror attacks.

Gyllenhaal, 27, made the comments at the Tribeca Film Festival, where her new movie "The Great New Wonderful" — which has a plot centered on the destruction of the World Trade Center — premiered Friday.

"I think what's good about the movie is that it deals with 9/11 in such a subtle, open, open way that I think it allows it to be more complicated than, 'Oh, look at these poor New Yorkers and how hard it was for them,'" Gyl-

Gyllenhaal

lenhaal told the New York 1 cable channel.

"Because I think America has done reprehensible things and is responsible in some way and so I think the delicacy with which it's dealt allows that to sort of creep in," she added.

A lower East Side native, Gyllenhaal's new film focuses on a handful of New Yorkers coping with their pain about a year after the Sept. 11, 2001, terror strike.

The actress vaulted to stardom after appearing in "Secretary" as a mousy assistant.

The film festival where Gyllenhaal spoke was launched by actor Robert De Niro in 2002 as a way to help scarred lower Manhattan rebound.

mhaberman@...

Summit in Brazil at odds with U.S.

BRASILIA — South American and Arab leaders at their first regional summit endorsed a declaration yesterday condemning the Israeli occupation of Palestinian territory. The countries are staking out positions at odds with U.S. policy on several fronts while committing to closer political and economic ties for the two far-flung regions.

Jailed journalist freed

A freelance videographer walked out of federal prison yesterday after spending more time behind bars than any other journalist for refusing to obey a subpoena to turn over his videotape of a chaotic 2005 San Francisco street protest during the G-8 summit.

Joshua Wolf, 24, posted online the unaired videotape that he had refused to give federal authorities, defense lawyer David Greene said yesterday. (AP)

Wolf

Israel apartheid flap

GENEVA — An independent report commissioned by the UN compares Israel's actions in the West Bank and Gaza Strip to apartheid in South Africa — charges that have drawn angry rebukes from Israel. The report by a South African lawyer says, "Israel's laws and practices... certainly resemble aspects of apartheid."

Where's Castro?
Students hold Cuban flags and a picture of revolutionary leader Ernesto "Che" Guevara yesterday during the May Day parade in Havana. There was no sign of a convalescing Fidel Castro as hundreds of thousands marched through Revolution Plaza to celebrate an event Castro had attended for decades without fail. (AP)

Newspaper Clips:
New York Daily News
AM News
New York Post
New York Times
Associated Press

DJ DEEP FREEZE

Seth "Soul Man" Ferranti
www.gorillaconvict.com

In the world of Hip Hop, artists are only as legit as their latest arrest. With the street culture influencing and maximizing credibility, every rapper and DJ wants to be down. In the hood, on the block, in the penitentiaries ... its all relative; a surefire recipe to success. And since most rappers are middlemen, studio gangstas per say, why not cut out the middleman and bring the streets right to the listeners. This is what DJ Deep Freeze and Sub Z-ro Entertainment has done with their Speak to the Streets mixtape series which features the words and stories of some of New York City's most infamous and notorious drug lords. "I knew these men were dying to speak out and live again," DJ Deep Freeze says. He refers to street legends such as Guy Fisher, Boy George, Akbar Pray, Chaz Williams, Lance Feurtado and Jack Frost who told their often violent and murderous tales on mixtapes set between tracks by 50 Cent, Fat Joe and the Game, among others.

"I asked these legends to speak to the streets. Teach the youth." he explains. "I made them aware that they were the epitome of gangsta and that there are many who still try to mimic and live up to and live out the now-bloated stories, either in reality or through rap." DJ Deep Freeze is no stranger to the penal system himself.

"I'm from Harlem World New York," he says. "I'm 36 years old and been rapping and DJ-ing since I was a kid, but unfortunately jail took my best years and ruined my rap dreams." But through his mixtapes, DJ Deep Freeze is gaining notoriety and giving a forum on a musical level for New York street legends to speak and let it be known that the fast lane isn't all that.

"I decided to go to these gangsta drug lords and have these men speak to the streets. I wanted to wake my people up. For some reason, we believe being gangsta, killing one another and selling drugs to achieve success is what's happening." And if the youth won't heed the words of an O.G., then who will they listen too?

But DJ Deep Freeze has more plans. "My company, Sub Z-ro Entertainment, has already graduated from the audio to the visual," he says. "We're now doing Hip Hop/street DVDs." And just like that, he has made the jump, but he gives props where props are due.

"I'd like to thank Guy Fisher, Boy George, Chaz Williams, the Feurtado Brothers, Akbar Pray and John Cuff for giving me my start to a positive success."

And there it is a man showing respect to those who deserve it: Gangsta royalty. Others in the world of Hip Hop should learn as much.

ICED ASSED OUT

by Euriah X. Bennett

*"Some people want diamond rings
Some just want everything
But everything means nothing
If I ain't got you".* - Alicia Keys

How the Bling-Bling Mindset is Destroying the Motherland

Ms. Keys sings a lovely song as she expresses the deeper meaning of love. As the song goes, she would much rather have her man by her side than a superficial diamond ring on her finger. As a member of the hip-hop generation and a popular artist, her expressions run counter to the prevalent mindset among hip-hop artists today. While Alicia expresses the importance of love beyond material things, other artists and performers express their love FOR material things.

Everyone knows the song "Bling Bling" by the Hot Boys. The song was a leading party starter for the summer of 2000. Over four years later it still moves the crowd. Furthermore, the unashamedly materialistic lyrics and infectious beat caught on with the larger American culture as well. Now, the word "bling" is actually in the dictionary. There is even a book titled *Bling*.

Hip-hop's love affair with diamonds and materialism continues. We hear Ludacris rapping that the chain around his neck is the size of a midget. According to a special aired on VH-1 in the summer of 2004, Jay-Z wears a diamond covered watch worth $700,000. Diamond encrusted teeth are everywhere. Lil Jon's teeth are worth $80,000. Baby, Master P and Nelly all have very expensive diamond encrusted teeth. And, of course, there are the goblets. Goblets owned by Lil Jon, Snoop Dogg and 50-Cent are encrusted with diamonds. The symbol that reps the crew or the label must have an emblem that is incrusted with diamonds like the G-Unit symbol, Lil Jon's CRUNKED, Kanye West's Jesus pieces and Nelly's #1.

Rappers lyrically espouse their desire for diamond jewelry, and flash diamond jewelry in their videos, some of which are only props used to convey a status that the rappers have yet to attain. Their craving for and purchase of "iced-out" status symbols have an obviously high dollar price. Sadly, there is a human price attached to diamonds. The hip-hop community rarely reflects on how the diamond trade negatively affects African communities and perpetuates the status quo of colonialism in various African countries.

"Ours was not a civil war. It was not a war based on ideology, religion or ethnicity, nor was it a 'class war.' It was a war of proxy aimed at permanent rebel control of our rich diamond fields for the benefit of outsiders."

— Ahmad Tejan Kabbah, President of Sierra Leone

The Diamond Life in Sierra Leone

From 1991 to 2000, the African country of Sierra Leone, located on the western coast of Africa has suffered from a brutal civil war, as forces fought over control of the country's diamond mines. The war, which began against the neo-colonial government, has wreaked havoc primarily on civilians. While the history of the neo-colonial governments within Sierra Leone have been marked by corruption since 1991 the Revolutionary United Front (RUF) primarily pillaged the country for its diamond wealth. Soldiers of the RUF were known for their horrific amputations of hands, feet, lips, ears and noses. The RUF terrorized the civilian population to ensure that the masses would not support the current government and to promote induction into the RUF. Children and women were targeted to heighten the terror. In fact, in 1999, the prime minister of Sierra Leone brought a little girl to a United Nations discussion on the problems within Sierra Leone. The girl's hands had been chopped off. Since 1991, the war has claimed nearly 100,000 lives, caused over a half a million natives of Sierra Leone to become refugees and displaced half of the country's 4.5 million people (Source: The Heart of the Matter: Sierra Leone, Diamonds & Human Security, Partnership Africa Canada, January 2000).

In spite of this, Sierra Leone's exploitation did not start with the deadly actions resulting from its civil war. Since the 1930s, European interests have exploited Sierra Leone's diamond wealth. The Sierra Leone Selection Trust (SLST), a British company operating on behalf of the colonial government, cotrolled much of the diamond wealth of Sierra Leone. While the enrichment of the colonial and European interests were obvious, the social-economic conditions of the people of Sierra Leone did not improve. Consequently, any diamond mining operation that operated outside of the machinations of the colonials were considered legitimate by the indigenous population (Source: War and Peace in Sierra Leone: Diamonds, Corruption and the Lebanese Connection, Lansana Gberie, p.7). The mining operations outside of the colonial interests were initially under the control of the Paramount Chief and Tribal Authority.

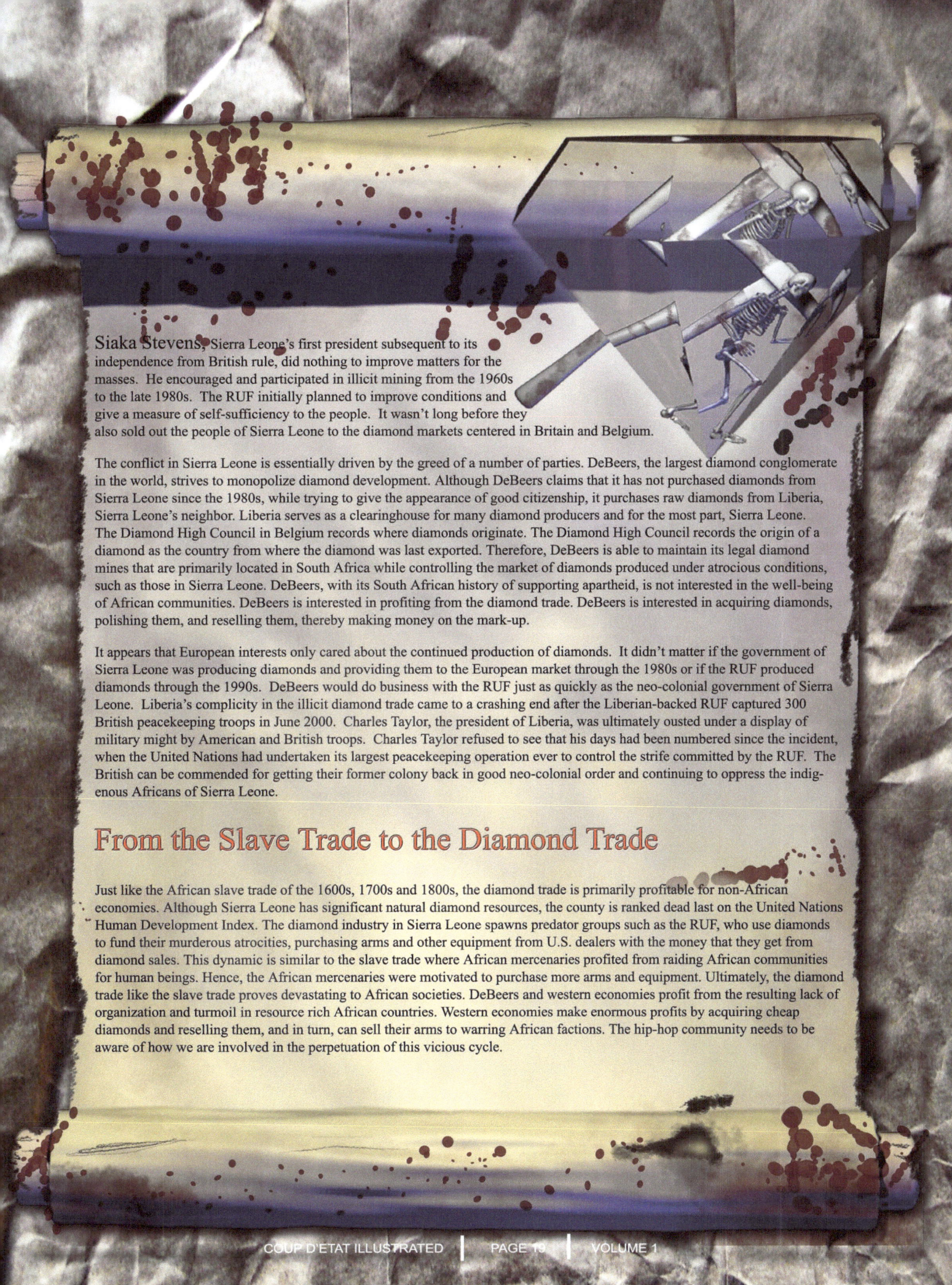

Siaka Stevens, Sierra Leone's first president subsequent to its independence from British rule, did nothing to improve matters for the masses. He encouraged and participated in illicit mining from the 1960s to the late 1980s. The RUF initially planned to improve conditions and give a measure of self-sufficiency to the people. It wasn't long before they also sold out the people of Sierra Leone to the diamond markets centered in Britain and Belgium.

The conflict in Sierra Leone is essentially driven by the greed of a number of parties. DeBeers, the largest diamond conglomerate in the world, strives to monopolize diamond development. Although DeBeers claims that it has not purchased diamonds from Sierra Leone since the 1980s, while trying to give the appearance of good citizenship, it purchases raw diamonds from Liberia, Sierra Leone's neighbor. Liberia serves as a clearinghouse for many diamond producers and for the most part, Sierra Leone. The Diamond High Council in Belgium records where diamonds originate. The Diamond High Council records the origin of a diamond as the country from where the diamond was last exported. Therefore, DeBeers is able to maintain its legal diamond mines that are primarily located in South Africa while controlling the market of diamonds produced under atrocious conditions, such as those in Sierra Leone. DeBeers, with its South African history of supporting apartheid, is not interested in the well-being of African communities. DeBeers is interested in profiting from the diamond trade. DeBeers is interested in acquiring diamonds, polishing them, and reselling them, thereby making money on the mark-up.

It appears that European interests only cared about the continued production of diamonds. It didn't matter if the government of Sierra Leone was producing diamonds and providing them to the European market through the 1980s or if the RUF produced diamonds through the 1990s. DeBeers would do business with the RUF just as quickly as the neo-colonial government of Sierra Leone. Liberia's complicity in the illicit diamond trade came to a crashing end after the Liberian-backed RUF captured 300 British peacekeeping troops in June 2000. Charles Taylor, the president of Liberia, was ultimately ousted under a display of military might by American and British troops. Charles Taylor refused to see that his days had been numbered since the incident, when the United Nations had undertaken its largest peacekeeping operation ever to control the strife committed by the RUF. The British can be commended for getting their former colony back in good neo-colonial order and continuing to oppress the indigenous Africans of Sierra Leone.

From the Slave Trade to the Diamond Trade

Just like the African slave trade of the 1600s, 1700s and 1800s, the diamond trade is primarily profitable for non-African economies. Although Sierra Leone has significant natural diamond resources, the county is ranked dead last on the United Nations Human Development Index. The diamond industry in Sierra Leone spawns predator groups such as the RUF, who use diamonds to fund their murderous atrocities, purchasing arms and other equipment from U.S. dealers with the money that they get from diamond sales. This dynamic is similar to the slave trade where African mercenaries profited from raiding African communities for human beings. Hence, the African mercenaries were motivated to purchase more arms and equipment. Ultimately, the diamond trade like the slave trade proves devastating to African societies. DeBeers and western economies profit from the resulting lack of organization and turmoil in resource rich African countries. Western economies make enormous profits by acquiring cheap diamonds and reselling them, and in turn, can sell their arms to warring African factions. The hip-hop community needs to be aware of how we are involved in the perpetuation of this vicious cycle.

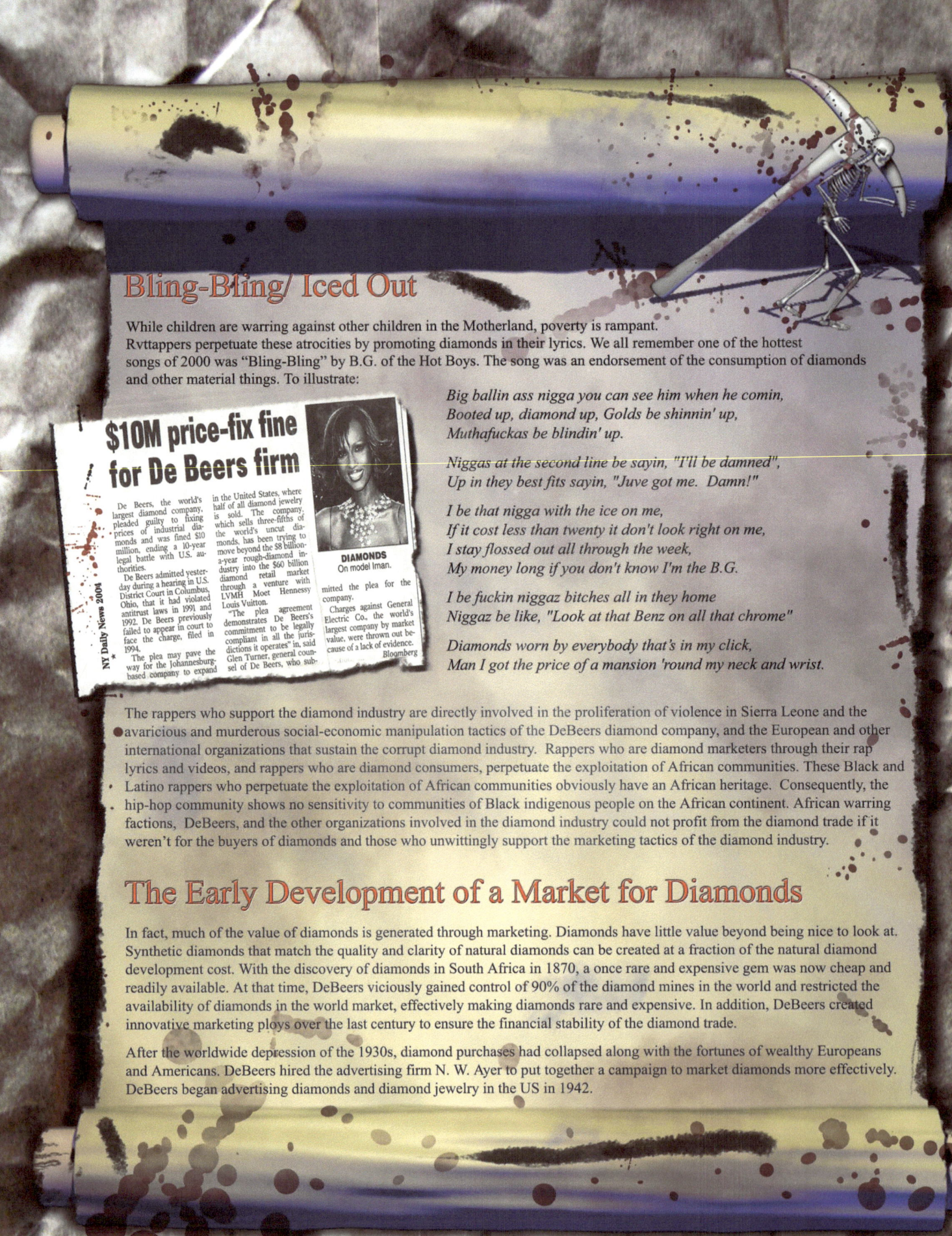

Bling-Bling/ Iced Out

While children are warring against other children in the Motherland, poverty is rampant. Rvttappers perpetuate these atrocities by promoting diamonds in their lyrics. We all remember one of the hottest songs of 2000 was "Bling-Bling" by B.G. of the Hot Boys. The song was an endorsement of the consumption of diamonds and other material things. To illustrate:

> Big ballin ass nigga you can see him when he comin,
> Booted up, diamond up, Golds be shinnin' up,
> Muthafuckas be blindin' up.
>
> Niggas at the second line be sayin, "I'll be damned",
> Up in they best fits sayin, "Juve got me. Damn!"
>
> I be that nigga with the ice on me,
> If it cost less than twenty it don't look right on me,
> I stay flossed out all through the week,
> My money long if you don't know I'm the B.G.
>
> I be fuckin niggaz bitches all in they home
> Niggaz be like, "Look at that Benz on all that chrome"
>
> Diamonds worn by everybody that's in my click,
> Man I got the price of a mansion 'round my neck and wrist.

$10M price-fix fine for De Beers firm

De Beers, the world's largest diamond company, pleaded guilty to fixing prices of industrial diamonds and was fined $10 million, ending a 10-year legal battle with U.S. authorities.

De Beers admitted yesterday during a hearing in U.S. District Court in Columbus, Ohio, that it had violated antitrust laws in 1991 and 1992. De Beers previously failed to appear in court to face the charge, filed in 1994.

The plea may pave the way for the Johannesburg-based company to expand in the United States, where half of all diamond jewelry is sold. The company, which sells three-fifths of the world's uncut diamonds, has been trying to move beyond the $8 billion-a-year rough-diamond industry into the $60 billion diamond retail market through a venture with LVMH Moet Hennessy Louis Vuitton.

"The plea agreement demonstrates De Beers's commitment to be legally compliant in all the jurisdictions it operates", said Glen Turner, general counsel of De Beers, who submitted the plea for the company.

Charges against General Electric Co., the world's largest company by market value, were thrown out because of a lack of evidence.
— Bloomberg

NY Daily News 2004

DIAMONDS On model Iman.

The rappers who support the diamond industry are directly involved in the proliferation of violence in Sierra Leone and the avaricious and murderous social-economic manipulation tactics of the DeBeers diamond company, and the European and other international organizations that sustain the corrupt diamond industry. Rappers who are diamond marketers through their rap lyrics and videos, and rappers who are diamond consumers, perpetuate the exploitation of African communities. These Black and Latino rappers who perpetuate the exploitation of African communities obviously have an African heritage. Consequently, the hip-hop community shows no sensitivity to communities of Black indigenous people on the African continent. African warring factions, DeBeers, and the other organizations involved in the diamond industry could not profit from the diamond trade if it weren't for the buyers of diamonds and those who unwittingly support the marketing tactics of the diamond industry.

The Early Development of a Market for Diamonds

In fact, much of the value of diamonds is generated through marketing. Diamonds have little value beyond being nice to look at. Synthetic diamonds that match the quality and clarity of natural diamonds can be created at a fraction of the natural diamond development cost. With the discovery of diamonds in South Africa in 1870, a once rare and expensive gem was now cheap and readily available. At that time, DeBeers viciously gained control of 90% of the diamond mines in the world and restricted the availability of diamonds in the world market, effectively making diamonds rare and expensive. In addition, DeBeers created innovative marketing ploys over the last century to ensure the financial stability of the diamond trade.

After the worldwide depression of the 1930s, diamond purchases had collapsed along with the fortunes of wealthy Europeans and Americans. DeBeers hired the advertising firm N. W. Ayer to put together a campaign to market diamonds more effectively. DeBeers began advertising diamonds and diamond jewelry in the US in 1942.

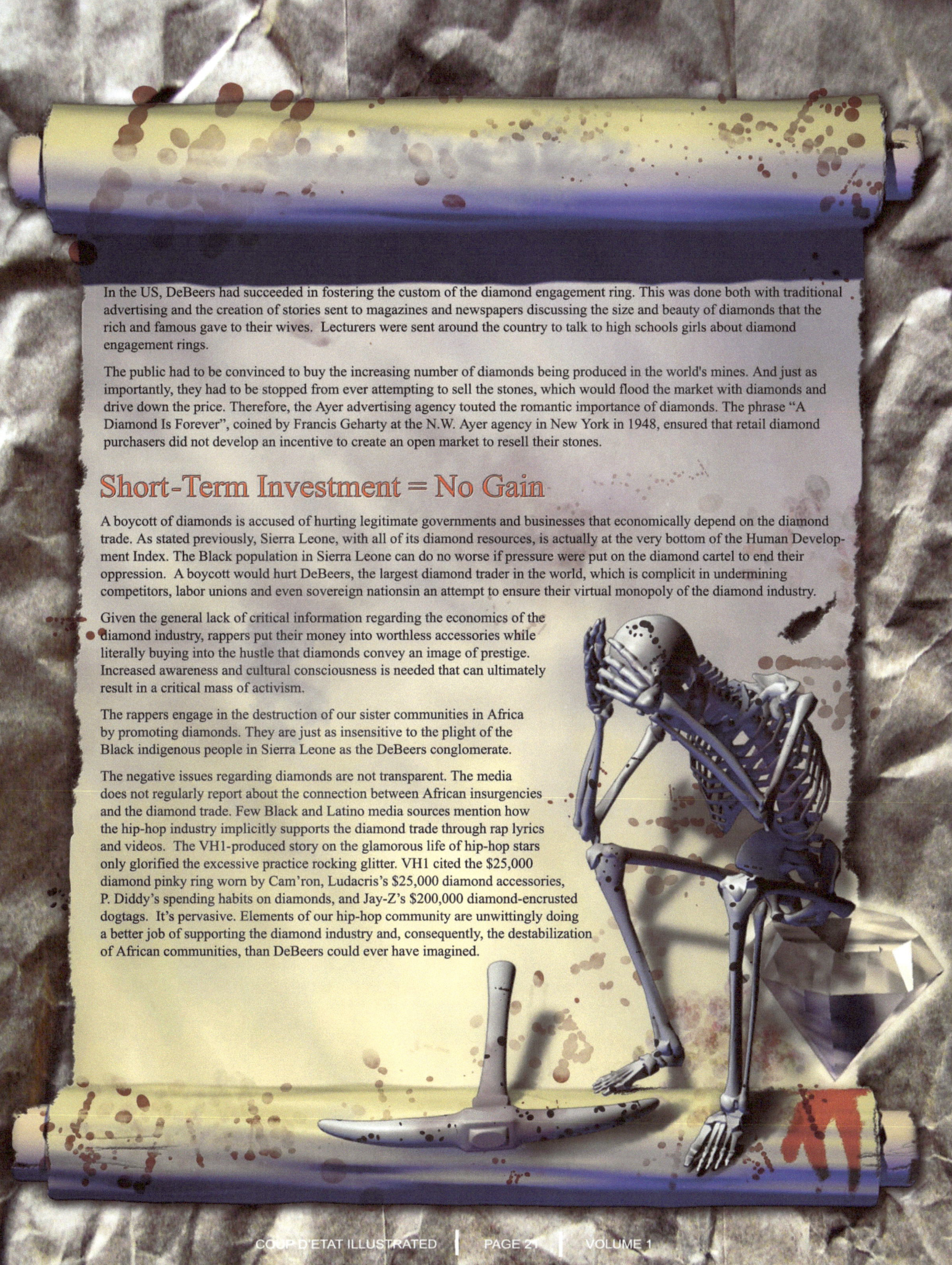

In the US, DeBeers had succeeded in fostering the custom of the diamond engagement ring. This was done both with traditional advertising and the creation of stories sent to magazines and newspapers discussing the size and beauty of diamonds that the rich and famous gave to their wives. Lecturers were sent around the country to talk to high schools girls about diamond engagement rings.

The public had to be convinced to buy the increasing number of diamonds being produced in the world's mines. And just as importantly, they had to be stopped from ever attempting to sell the stones, which would flood the market with diamonds and drive down the price. Therefore, the Ayer advertising agency touted the romantic importance of diamonds. The phrase "A Diamond Is Forever", coined by Francis Geharty at the N.W. Ayer agency in New York in 1948, ensured that retail diamond purchasers did not develop an incentive to create an open market to resell their stones.

Short-Term Investment = No Gain

A boycott of diamonds is accused of hurting legitimate governments and businesses that economically depend on the diamond trade. As stated previously, Sierra Leone, with all of its diamond resources, is actually at the very bottom of the Human Development Index. The Black population in Sierra Leone can do no worse if pressure were put on the diamond cartel to end their oppression. A boycott would hurt DeBeers, the largest diamond trader in the world, which is complicit in undermining competitors, labor unions and even sovereign nationsin an attempt to ensure their virtual monopoly of the diamond industry.

Given the general lack of critical information regarding the economics of the diamond industry, rappers put their money into worthless accessories while literally buying into the hustle that diamonds convey an image of prestige. Increased awareness and cultural consciousness is needed that can ultimately result in a critical mass of activism.

The rappers engage in the destruction of our sister communities in Africa by promoting diamonds. They are just as insensitive to the plight of the Black indigenous people in Sierra Leone as the DeBeers conglomerate.

The negative issues regarding diamonds are not transparent. The media does not regularly report about the connection between African insurgencies and the diamond trade. Few Black and Latino media sources mention how the hip-hop industry implicitly supports the diamond trade through rap lyrics and videos. The VH1-produced story on the glamorous life of hip-hop stars only glorified the excessive practice rocking glitter. VH1 cited the $25,000 diamond pinky ring worn by Cam'ron, Ludacris's $25,000 diamond accessories, P. Diddy's spending habits on diamonds, and Jay-Z's $200,000 diamond-encrusted dogtags. It's pervasive. Elements of our hip-hop community are unwittingly doing a better job of supporting the diamond industry and, consequently, the destabilization of African communities, than DeBeers could ever have imagined.

STREET DVD's

By: Seth "Soul Man" Ferranti
www.gorillaconvict.com

There is nothing slow about the streets, and the rap game has been quick to recognize. Crime has no color and a bullet has no name on it. The visual interpretation of the mix tapes craze and thug life magazines like Don Diva, FEDs, and As Is has made its way from the streets to your living room via the street DVD which has become the popular media outlet of the day. From inner city thugs looking to expose snitches, to Hip-Hop artists trying to keep it real, to gang bangers showing their bravado, to street savvy entrepreneurs who want to capitalize on urban legends and their stories, the new makers of street DVD's have broken into the game and brought it to a new level through the world of digital media.

The independently produced, distributed and marketed films come in the form of DVD magazines or video street journals like Smack, All Access, Cheddar, Cocaine City, Sub 0 Cold World and The Come Up; reality based and tell-all exposes like Ganglife, Hood2Hood and Stop Snitching; The Life of Rayful Edmond, The Original 50 Cent and Cocaine Cowboys or educational clips like King of Kings. Their mission is to shock, entertain, educate and captivate, and they have been doing their job as a lot of the independents have been picked up by majors.

"We were growing so big on an underground level that I felt we couldn't get any bigger through independent distribution," says Troy Mitchell, founder of Smack. And with the success of BET's American Gangster series, the medium is taking flight, but it wasn't always so. Troy Reed, who runs Street Stars, producers of The Guy Fisher Story, Game Over and The Alpo Story explains. "It was extremely difficult (at first) because nobody had DVD's like this in the stores." But now the films – which cost $15,000 to $25,000 to make – are in high demand.

"Many people were reading these stories in Don Diva and FEDs. We provide the video perspective," Troy says.

And with the established companies signing major deals, numerous new filmmakers are entering the marketplace with their version of the hood story of their respective city. Like Skinny Suge, who created the Stop Snitching DVD which made headlines due to an appearance by Carmelo Anthony, and DJ Deep Freeze who is causing controversy with the street violence at rap concerts in his Sub 0 Cold World DVD's.

"I want to wake my people up," DJ Deep Freeze says of the disturbing images in his Cold World DVD's. "For some reason we believe being gangsta and selling drugs to achieve success is what's happening. When all that's really happening is they're filling prisons with my people at an alarming rate."

And with the DVD's becoming promotional vehicles for rappers to air out their beefs – as in The Game's Stop Lying DVD aimed at 50 cent – the medium has become a valuable marketing tool. But others are using it to educate and take away the myths of the drug lords such as Lance Feurtado of Seven Crowns fame with his DVD King of Kings.

"The DVD is an educational documentary about the Feurtado Brothers (rise in the drug game). We are from the streets taking it back to the streets," he says.

Others, such as the infamous Calvin Klein Bacote of Jay-Z and Red Hook fame are literally coming out of prison, making DVDs and trying to capitalize off their notoriety. His documentary, The Story of the Brooklyn Don features interviews with Jimmy Henchman of Czar Entertainment, and Kevin Chiles of Don Diva magazine along with Calvin Klein's story in his own words.

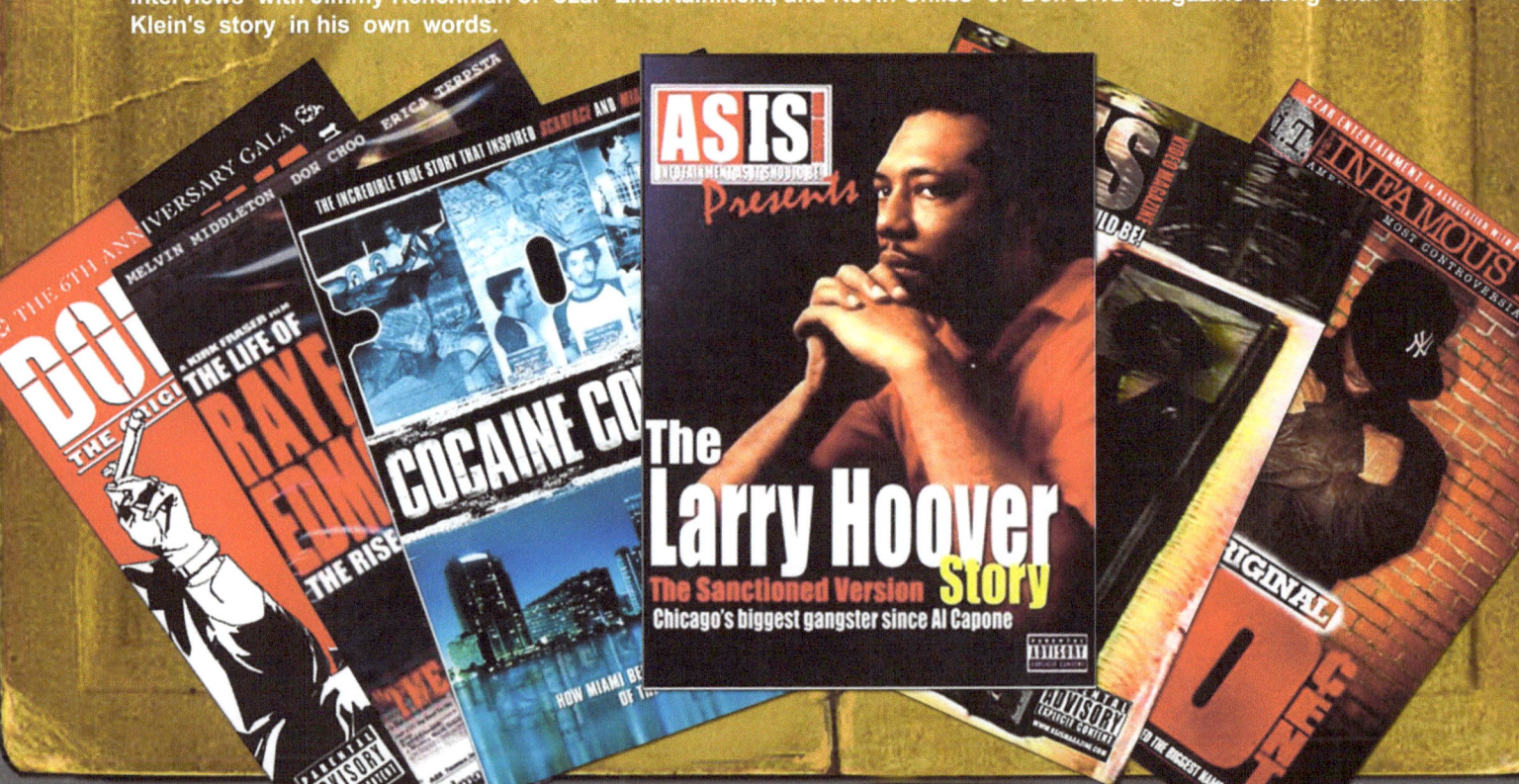

Graffiti Hall of Fame
By George "Squeeze" Morillo

2004 Graffiti Hall of Fame

On June 26, 2004 in a New York City public school yard located on 106th Street and Park Avenue, in the heart of Spanish Harlem, both young and old turned out for an event that has become a tradition for decades among true hip-hop lovers. Transforming an old, rural and decaying schoolyard into an urban art gallery by graffiti artists from all over the world. Hip-hop's oldest and most colorful element showcased why the art of graffiti will never die, no matter how many efforts are made to destroy it by the system.

Back in the early 1980s some of the best-known graffiti artists got together and created the "Graffiti Hall of Fame". This community project was developed to relieve some of the urban despair that most New Yorkers were experiencing at the time. In 1981, Graffiti artists "Dez" and "Vulcan" did the first outside wall on Park Avenue that welcomed all visitors. Inside the park, only artists who were declared "Kings" laid the first foundation of spray paint that would continue until this day. Some of the first graffiti artists, now legends, blessed us with their aliases. Among them were Futura, Skeme, Doze, Jon 156, and countless others who left their souls forever on those walls.

At the 2004 event, the legacy continued with the return of some of the old school veterans from the hip-hop underworld. In attendance were Bonz Malone, Lucky from Universal Zulu Nation, and Kurtis Blow. Some original B-Boys, like Ken Swift and Frosty Freeze from the Rock Steady Crew, were on hand as well. DJ KC was on the turntables while Dezzy Dez AKA DJ Kay Slay hosted the event. The headliners were the graffiti artists that came to rep, and for a moment live in the past when life was more simple and true hip-hop was everything. The artists who immersed their souls in this graffiti sanctuary for all to witness included Blake, Wen, TATS CRU, and many more who turned out to showcase their skills. The DJs added the musical link that makes hip-hop. The B-Boys and B-Girls battled each other, while dazzled spectators eyed their trademarked moves, so that one day they might use them against their own inventors. The MCs and the rappers were free-styling. The women put it down just as hard as their male counterparts, if not harder. We can't forget hip-hop's strong international family that came out not only to show support, but also to show their American cousins a thing or two.

The gates to this urban gallery are open all year round, and if you happen to be in New York City, make sure that you come and visit this cultural phenomenon. The Graffiti Hall of Fame is located in Spanish Harlem on 106th Street and Park Avenue. The event is usually held in June. It is very important to support hip-hop events like that at the Graffiti Hall of Fame, Zulu Nation's anniversary, the Rock Steady Crew's reunion, and Russell Simmons's Hip-Hop Summit so that we can keep the spirit of true hip-hop alive. Pick up our next issue to see the 2005 Graffiti Hall of Fame.

Frosty Freeze & Ken Swift
"Rock Steady Crew"

DJ Kay Slay/Dezzy Dez
The Graffiti Hall of Fame 2004

CDI recently caught up with the drama king himself, DJ Kay Slay at the Graffiti Hall of Fame in NYC. DJ Kay Slay was once known in the world of hip-hop as Dezzy Dez, a street-famed graffiti writer, and now he's a major force in the rap industry and in the world of mix tapes. Some of you might have gotten your first glimpse of Dez in the classic underground graffiti documentary "Style Wars," and some of you might just know him as DJ Kay Slay who brought us the recent classic rap battles, like Nas and Jay Z. Kay Slay has brought back the competitive creativity of early hip-hop battles to the rap game. So we decided to ask DJ Kay Slay to grade the new graffiti covering these sacred walls.

DJ Kay Slay: The shit is right; you know what I'm saying. I ain't mad, there's a lot of motherfuckers that I don't know down here, but outside of that it's all hip-hop man. The first element of hip-hop is graffiti, you know what I'm saying. Everybody came out to show love and have a good time and it's all gravy. I'm keeping it real on all that.

2Pac, Jam Master Jay, Big L, B.I.G., & Big Pun R.I.P.

KURTIS BLOW & FRIENDS

CDI: How do you describe being a rap pioneer that struggled back in the early days of hip-hop when radio wouldn't even play it, and now having so many people exploiting it—this is regarding those individuals that had nothing to do with the original creation and who are now capitalizing on it today?

Kurtis Blow: First, we as the elderly spokesmen, have to stay positive because WE ARE THE PIONEERS. We're the guys that actually made it possible so that the younger generation could make the money that they are making today. So we can't be frustrated, angry or upset at all the things that were going down. We have to be happy and truly, truly elated and walk around with our heads up high, because we created it. We made the avenue for kids to come along and make the dollars that they're making now. So my God, I WAS THERE FROM THE BEGINNING. I experienced the Kool Herc and DJ Jones parties and I know the difference between the two. So that's something that I hold dear in my heart that no one can take away from me. So, all of my peers I want to talk to them, you guys should not be frustrated, show love to all the younger kids that are out there today. Show them the way to go, you know what I mean. Because it's our job right now, we are the elderly spokesmen, we have to keep it real, keep it clean, keep it good, keep it positive, shine a light so that everybody else can rub off on that light and make it happen. Only then it will continue, not die, only multiply.

NATIONAL CONFERENCE OF BLACK MAYORS DOIN' BIG THANGS

Peoples, it went down when the 31st National Conference of Black Mayors took over Columbus Ohio this April, promising to be nothing less than exciting with a roster that included some of the most influential Black folk in politics and entertainment. And just like Fed Ex, it delivered. Start to finish, the conference was enlightening and inspiring. From Vivica Fox and

Reported by **Avis Skinner**, The Intelligent Hoodlum

Fox and Cecily Tyson to dead prez and Farrakhan, the kaleidoscope of Black dignitaries covered the entire spectrum—all coming together to show some love.

For those who don't know, there are over 500 Black mayors in this country, representing both small and large populated areas. These mayors meet once a year; handing out scholarships, holding meetings that address the mounting issues that plague our community, and working together to find solutions to those issues. It was also a celebration of those Black Americans who have worked to make a difference, not only in their community, but for communities of color across the globe. This year, the 2005 NCBM, no doubt, will go down in history. Check it, here's your play-by-play.

DAY 1 - THE JUMP OFF

The first day started with a press conference, allowing members of the media to pose questions to the mayors about topics to be discussed during the course of this year's event. Off the rip, racism had to be addressed, because as we learned during the conference, it is still a dark, looming cloud over this country's patriotic, blue skies. Especially when it comes to the distribution of government funding. "We're saying these things [racial discrimination] exist, even though we in America say they don't. And our communities suffer because of this." said Mayor Irene Brodie, of Robbins Illinois. "We're denied opportunities very often. We don't have money to run our communities if we don't have commerce."

We've all heard the tales of Black Americans having to be twice as good as their White counterparts when it comes to jobs and promotions. Black politicians are no different. "The bar is always raised. We always have to be squeaky clean. We have to be better than. We just can't go and do our jobs. So every day is a challenge," Mayor Floyd Griffin, Jr. of Milledgeville Georgia explains. "Not only in White communities, but in Black communities as well."

NCBM president, Mayor Roosevelt Dorn of Inglewood California, was painfully optimistic when he got his shot at the mic, "Rather than using that [race] as an excuse, what we've learned to do is take advantage and use it in a positive manner." He continued, "Communication is the key. Unless we have dialogue, we'll always have these problems."

DAY 2 - NO, WE WON'T SHUT UP!

Dead prez literally stopped the show at the Youth Day Celebration. After Ludacris and Mos Def were unable to make it, dead prez stepped up only to get shut down. When the group began spitting controversial lyrics that implied that Bin Ladin was trained by the CIA, one of the board members rushed to the soundmen and told them they were finished. When I asked why, I got no response. It doesn't take a rocket scientist to figure out that their lyrics were too controversial for the event. Black or not, [the mayors] are still politicians.

Despite the mics being cut off, dead prez continued with their message of liberation. Telling the high school seniors to protect themselves, their family and their communities, be organized and for each one to teach one.

Mr. Benjamin Chavis

DAY 3 - KNOWLEDGE REIGNS SUPREME

As each day passed, it left its mark on the just the conference, but the city of Columbus and the people who attended, just like myself. And this day was no different.

Fannie Lou Hamer, an activist who fought for the voting rights of Black folk during the

> When I asked why, I got no response. It doesn't take a rocket scientist to figure out that their lyrics were too controversial for the event. Black or not, they are still politicians.

NATIONAL CONFERENCE OF BLACK MAYORS DOIN' BIG THANGS

M1 & Stic (dead prez) performance

Stic & M1 (dead prez)

Vivica Fox

Who'll Be Seen With Howard Dean?

civil rights movement, was the inspiration behind the award given at a luncheon during the conference. This award, for the NCBM represents achievement, power and revolution. And this year's recipient of the Fannie Lou Hamer Freedom Award was hip-hop mogul Russell Simmons.

Simmons, who has 34 companies, was unable to attend. But, this was no setback, ladies and gentlemen. Mr. Benjamin Chavis, who works closely with Simmons through his Hip-Hop Summit Action Network, was on hand to accept the award for him. Big ups to Mr. Chavis, as in the movie *Belly*, he didn't let us down. "This generation is the best generation of youth that we've ever had. They're our best! This generation of youth has the weight of many different problems that they're born into, in our community. And so this generation doesn't need so much the pointing finger of what is wrong with young people. What this generation needs is our helping hand. Our embrace. Our love. Our support. Our nurturing and our leadership."

I cannot go on without talking about the think tank that included the Honorable Minister Louis Farrakhan and Dr. Manning Marable, (Columbia University, New York City). The topic for the think tank was the Triad of color-blind racism—Mass Unemployment, Mass Incarceration and Mass Disenfranchisement.

"Nationwide, for the last 30 years, the number of people in U.S. jails and prisons has risen from 200,000 to 2.2 million. Mandatory minimum sentencing laws adopted in the 80's and 90's in these states, strip judges of discretionary powers in sentencing, imposing draconian terms on first-time and nonviolent offenders. Parole has been made much more restrictive all over the country. And in 1995, Pell grant subsidiaries supporting educational programs for prisoners were ended. For those fortunate enough to successfully navigate the criminal justice system, to move beyond and get out of prison, they've discovered that both the federal and state governments explicitly prohibit the employment of convicted former prisoners in literally hundreds of locations. The cycle of unemployment begins," Dr. Marable explained.

Did you know one out of five Americans has a criminal record? And it's not just Black people! The prison industrial complex is a billion-dollar industry. It's a revolving door, as one goes out, another goes in. It brings in millions of people every year. What part of the game is that? Human Capital, it gets deep ya'll.

They did put it down, calling for unity in our communities and the need to move past our "petty differences." That's some real "ish" right there.

DAY 4 – PAYING TRIBUTE TO A HOLLYWOOD LEGEND

Cicely Tyson, best known for her performance as Jane Pitman, was honored at the conference's "Tribute to a Black American" dinner. Mistress of Ceremonies was none other than Ms. Vivica A. Fox. And let me tell ya'll, both women looked absolutely gorgeous. Two generations of

NATIONAL CONFERENCE OF BLACK MAYORS DOIN' BIG THANGS

our society, stood side by side on the stage representin' for all those who said a sista couldn't do it for themselves. (All my ladies, who are independent, throw ya hands up at me.)

For those who don't know, Cecily Tyson, was Richard Pryor's love interest in *Bustin' Loose* (remember the school bus). She was the teacher who took care of the children. That is one of the things that is so great about Ms. Tyson. As an actress, she can do comedy and drama, both without effort. With a countless number of award nominations and some awards too, she is truly an inspiration to any actor/actress.

And not only is she an exceptional actress, she is a humanitarian. She has a performing arts school where she visits often named after her in New Jersey, which boast a graduation rate of 95%.

During her acceptance speech, Ms. Tyson, expressed her gratitude to the mayors and advised them, she quoted Jane Pitman ya'll, "I'm a urge you to keep on." Judging by the audience's reaction, this was the highlight of the evening.

From beginning to end, this year's conference, was...well, too many things. I'm going to close out this piece just as dead prez closed out their show, "embrace revolutionary love" ya'll. I'm feelin' that. Respect.

Mayor Roosevelt Dorn (NCBM president), Cecily Tyson, & Vivica Fox

(side bar)
Authors note: The night of dead prez's performance, a WSYX/WTTE (ABC affiliate, Colmbus, OH.) newscast reported that the group was swearing and said "f*** the police". There was no profanity. What prompted the abrupt closure of the show was the comment about Bin Ladin being trained by the CIA. I contacted M-1 of dead prez and he confirmed this. The group did not use profanity.

(side bar) dead prez Interview
These cats are some of the realest I've met in a while. They are strong, focused and true to the struggle. Even after being silenced, following their performance they signed autographs for students and took the time to speak to your girl.

Peoples, their critics want you to believe that these brothas are angry racists. As M-1 explains, this couldn't be further from the truth. "You can't mistake Black people's or African people's aspirations for freedom as any kind of hate-filled slogan. You have to recognize it as our truest effort and campaign for our own power and freedom, which is most important to us. We put it right beside our mothers' lives, our children's lives, and our future. It [freedom] is everything to us."

"I have a right to defend myself, verbally, politically, culturally, spiritually. Everybody's got that right." Stic addresses the faultfinders who claim they [dead prez] are too aggressive. "That doesn't make me more militant than George Bush in Iraq."

Appropriately enough, M-1 also touched on politicians and accountability, a sensitive topic in light of the occasion. "A lot of times the mayors are not accountable to the people and their issues. The people can't trust the leadership because our leadership is too wishy-washy. It blows any which ways the wind blows. We need true leadership that can be accountable and responsible."

Always a tense subject for any revolutionary, police brutality is at the forefront of the struggles of the hip-hop generation. "That's one of the frustrations we have as a community. The fear that the government has consistently put on our people through the police force." Stic expresses respect for the Black Panther Party and its ability to take care of problematic issues in a manner that was not destructive to the Black community. "A lot of them (Black Panthers) are still sitting in jail right now."

Keeping in step with their five points, dead prez not only talk the talk, they walk the walk. As a part of the Grassroots Artist Movement (G.A.M.e), they champion artists' rights to medical benefits and ownership of their material. G.A.M.e. is a union for artists—The hip-hop community's teamsters. Located in the birthplace of hip-hop, it seeks to reap the benefits for the real producers of hip-hop, the artists. **(To contact G.A.M.e send an email to info@kick-game.com)**

When I asked dead prez if their, in-your-face lyrics hurt their sales, they really weren't that pressed about it. "These sacrifices are most important to us because our principals matter more than money. We do have to eat but we won't compromise our principals," M-1 responded. Big ups to the pair of hip-hop activists, all movements entail sacrifice and few people are willing.

As I'm sure you've guessed by now, this wasn't the revolutionary duo's first time getting' shut down and I suspect it won't be the last. But as long as dead prez are holdin' the people down, the people are going to hold dead prez down. Respect.

(side bar) Mr. Benjamin Chavis Interview
After the Fannie Lou Hamer luncheon, I had the chance to speak with Mr. Ben Chavis. I asked him about what he thought about the previous day's events with HSAN artists, dead prez. He had this to say, "We should support freedom of expression, freedom of artistic expression. We just celebrated the Fannie Lou Hamer Freedom Award. The freedoms we fought for we also have to protect. And of course with freedom, comes responsibility." He went on to say, that he thought it was unfortunate, "if you give the young people time, they will make a profound statement. Rather than taking the mics from our young people, we need to be giving them more mics. We need to listen to our young people more." Shout out to Mr. Chavis, you definitely represent for the hip-hop generation and audience. Mad Love.

THE FUTURE OF HIP HOP

Rap, as we all know, had it's humble beginnings in "ghettos" across this country—an artistic expression of the angst's that plagued black, latino, and poor White youths' in America. A generation raised by oppression, poverty and Reganomics. Rap was an outlet for those of us who had no other way for our voices to be heard. With the birth and success of rap, a generation was able to stand up ad be counted. It wasn't just a life-style. It was a way of life. This is how we livin'! And there is no shame in our game. But now, those days are long forgotten. Rap has matured into hip-hop. It's not just rappin'. It's acting, modeling. It's journalism. And now, it's politics. It's official. Hip-hop is a "culture". Because of its ability to influence, politicians have taken notice. And because of its ability to turn a dollar, big corporate giants have taken over. Seduced by million dollar contracts and the opportunity for an honest hustle, a generation has switched gears to grind mode. We are hustlin' to eat. We are hustlin' to pay back our parents, to show them how grateful we are that they did the best they could, under the circumstances. We are hustlin' for our children, to offer them another way. We are hustlin' because we've grown accustomed to a certain lifestyle, and we've got to grind like hell to maintain it. The payoff has arrived. But why hasn't the quality of life gotten any better? We're hungrier than ever. The generation that was going to change the world only mimicked it. If we don't stop grindin' and start changin', Hip-Hop will die. It will die a slow, painful death, just as all fads and trends do. Rap will be the metal rock of our generation. If hip-hop is to survive this Bush Era (which is only a repeat of the Reagan Era), as a culture and a generation, we as a people must remain true to our vision of change. The music will live forever. Rap itself, will never die. The future of hip-hop reconnect with purpose and represents. I believe in hip-hop. I'm gonna hold you down…no doubt!!! Respect

AVIS SKINNER –

HIP-HOP JOURNALIST

NATIONAL CONFERENCE OF BLACK MAYORS DOIN' BIG THANGS

(side bar) Mama Cha Cha Interview

Mama Cha Cha, a faculty member of Columbus Afrocentric School, and several students attended the Youth Day Luncheon where dead prez performed. Admittedly not a rap fan, she says she was not offended by the performance at all. "That was the first time I heard dead prez and I really enjoyed it. I didn't find anything wrong with it." When I asked her, did she recall if the group used profanity, she said no. "That's something they [the youth] needed to hear." Not only is Mama Cha Cha considering buying one of the groups LP's, she said the doors to the school are open to the group, should they return to Columbus.

Audience Members

Editorial:

It strikes me as odd that for four days I heard how important it was to give our youth role models that they can emulate. So, when dead prez was treated like a couple of stepchildren, I was disappointed. Yet again, upper middleclass Black America has opted to disown the youth and the poverty stricken. During the think thank with Farrakhan, the honorable minister reached out to the mayors and told them that he understood what they go through. It is not easy being in their position and this is obviously something the constituents like myself would not comprehend. So now I understand why they cut the mics off on dead prez. They had to. But why then did they not tell the truth. That it was NOT because of the use of profanity, but because of the remarks made about President Bush, Bin Ladin and the CIA. dead prez would have respected the truth. Instead, these young brothers, are not only trying to feed themselves and their families, but also they are attempting to make a difference in their communities and in the world, they felt disrespected and abandoned by their own peoples. It was sad really. That day, I saw the generation gap widen, and I didn't think that was possible. I agree with Minister Farrakhan when he said, we must ignore our petty differences. Unity…for the Black community and for mankind. One love.

THE UNDERWORLD

Max Ginsburg's paintings are about people, the people one finds on the street of New York. Simply put, he finds beauty in unglamorous reality. His paintings explore the range of daily human life, concerned as much with life's ironies and social injustices, as with its many joys. He paints people that he can identify with, real people with regular lives. Although he attended art schools his real mentor was his father. Abraham Ginsburg was a successful portrait painter who taught Max the skills needed to paint in the traditional, realist manner, and kindled within him a love of realism that would shape his work for the rest of his life.

Over the years Max Ginsburg has had many one man shows and participated in many group shows in which he has won awards. During his career he has had to rely on teaching art and illustrating to earn a living. In his classes he taught and inspired students to draw and paint from life, to work in the tradition of the old masters, and more importantly, to think of art as a personal and deep expression of one's own ideas. Generations of students have gone on to excel as artists and art teachers; Ginsburg has taken tremendous joy in their achievements. One of Max Ginsburg student's whom went on to achieve greatness in the art world is Coup D'Etat Illustrated every own co-creator and illustrator Ricky Mujica.

Max Ginsburg
Email: info@maxginsburg.com
www.maxginsburg.com

Title: "BASKETBALL"
Dimensions: 41" x 44"
Medium: Oils

Title: "FIELD TRIP"   Dimensions: 20" x 30"   Medium: Oils

Title: "PARK BENCH"   Dimensions: 20" x 30"   Medium: Oils

Title: "NANNIES & KIDS"
Dimensions: 40" x 32"
Medium: Oils

Title: "TIRE SWING"
Dimensions: 36" x 36"
Medium: Oils

Title: "FLAG VENDOR"
Dimensions: 42" x 60"
Medium: Oils

Title: "HEBREW NATIONAL"
Dimensions: 36" x 46"
Medium: Oils

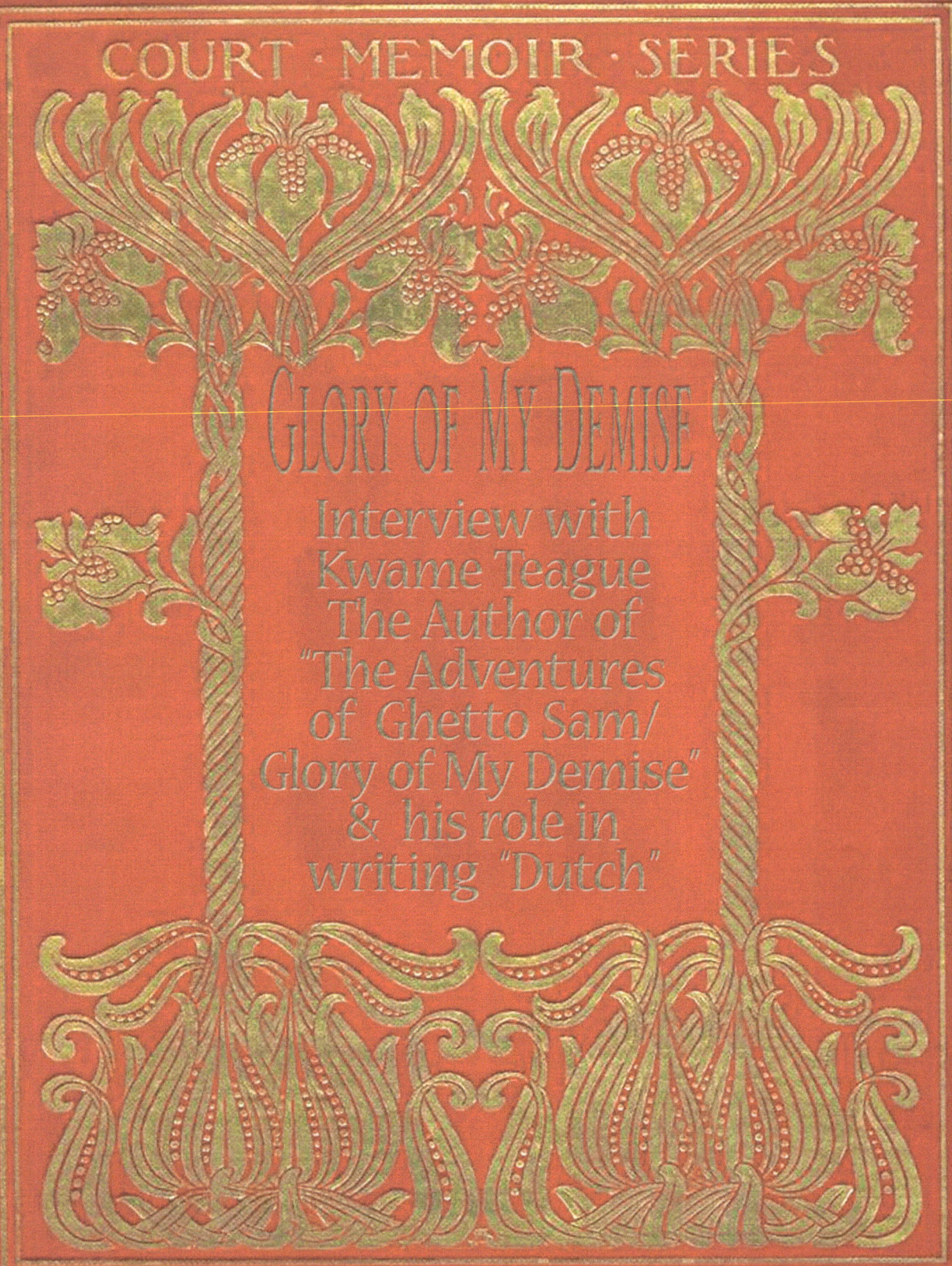

During the last two decades I have walked across 125th Street in Harlem and stopped at every bookstand, scouring the tables for literature. I gradually expanded my political library, buying books on history and revolutionaries.

At times I needed an emotional escape from the painful and enraging words of George Jackson *Soledad Brother* and *Assata* by Assata Shakur, so on occasion I snatched up a Donald Goines joint or an Iceberg Slim novel. These books were just as powerful and moving as the books that had given me a political "re-education".

As the years went by, the books on those tables in Harlem began to change. Urban romance novels and modern-day street crime stories, quickly took the places of Malcolm X and Bobby Seale's *Seize The Time* forcing me to spend my money at Barnes & Noble.

It seemed that many of the Black-owned independent bookstores were going out of business. A good friend of mine came to me one day and asked if I would do an interview with one of modern-day authors. As an aspiring writer I accepted. He gave me a book called *The Advetures of Ghetto Sam/Glory of My Demise* by Kwame Teague, and I remembered seeing it on many tables, but in my sometimes (well a lot of times!) hostile and judge-mental way, I always ignored it thinking, "I aint got time for that bullshit."

So I began to correspondence with Kwame Teague by while, reading his book simultaneously. It was a well-deserved and calculated body shot that harshly reminded me to never judge a book by its cover. It was articulate and brilliantly written, and, by comparison, made those big-selling urban novels seem sophomoric.

Kwame Teague is doing double life in prison and his second book *Dutch* is currently rocking the streets and then some.

Here is his voice, raw and uncut.

CDI: Why were you incarcerated?
KT: I was convicted in 1994 of double murder and sentenced to 2 life sentences. I maintain my innocence and I have been fighting for my freedom since my trial. That is the "black and white" of why I am locked up, but the underlying and chief causes are race, poverty, and the lack of good lawyers. Basically, the same reasons the majority of Black men are locked up, but the pain and frustration is compounded by my innocence. Imagine being picked up and charged by the police with a crime such as murder and not being able to defend yourself because no one is listening! The court system says that you are innocent until proven guilty but in the minds of the public (from which jurors are picked) the mere fact that you are charged implies guilt. You don't need much evidence because the people feel like he must be guilty of something or else no one would accuse him, especially not our judicial system, they wouldn't make such errors on purpose. To acknowledge that the system could convict an innocent man implies all innocent people could be charged and that would destroy the fiber of belief in the system period. To admit that our government could err so blatantly would mean no one is safe from this type of persecution. So people turn away from truth and hide behind the illusion of law. But those who are familiar with the injustice of the system are usually struck from juror pools, the jury of our peers the law is supposed to afford us, the state usually dismisses them because they can understand the truth. I can't talk about the particulars of my case, but anyone who is interested can contact ktproject@bellsouth.net and I can go into more detail.

CDI: What do you think would help you come home?
KT: The people. I don't need people to help in establishing my innocence that is already established. I need people to say to the state, how are you holding this man with no evidence only the word of a mentally unstable informant? Give him a fair trial, let us decide if he is guilty as you say. If he is, may God have mercy on his soul. If he isn't, may God have mercy on yours because this is not JUSTICE. I could be your brother., your husband, your son, father or friend. Would you sit idly by if this was happening to your loved ones? What makes you think your loved ones can't be next? Injustice anywhere threatens justice everywhere.

CDI: When did you first become interested in writing?
KT: About 11 or 12. My older sister, Sharon, taught me how to write in stage play format and I took off from there. At first, all I wrote was screenplays, which is my strongest format. I didn't write a book until 1999. That was my first attempt at writing a book. But I felt it was my only way of being heard from behind all this steel and concrete. But I didn't want to write an appeal, so to speak. I didn't want to take you inside the alleged crime of Kwame but inside the mind of Kwame. I wanted to be on more intimate terms with the reader and let them take the initiative in asking, "Why are you locked up?" Instead of proving why I shouldn't.

CDI: How many books have you had published?
KT: So far, two. *The Adventures of Ghetto Sam/Glory of My Demise* [2 books in one] and *Dutch*.

CDI: You say *Dutch*, but wasn't Teri Woods' name on the book as the writer, why?
KT: That was a marketing decision. *Ghetto Sam* established my audience as hip-hop type readers. It's probably the only book written really in the hip-hop vernacular, so unless you're totally immersed in that culture, you may not understand it. But *Dutch* is gangsta, true and uncut. One of the rawest, gangsta joints ever written, if not the rawest. This trilogy will set the standard for gangsta novel, like *Godfather* did in its day. So since Teri already had a "gangsta" audience (true to the game) it made sense to put her name on it. And like I say in *Dutch*, "they can't stop what they can't see."

CDI: What is your relationship with Teri and is she assisting you in your Fight for Freedom?

KT: My relationship with Teri is good. It's based on publisher/writer but she has gone out of her way several times to help me. The problem isn't her sincerity it's in her commitment, and that's because she doesn't understand my plight and what it'll take to address it. She writes in articles how she's down for cats in prison, and she has employed a few prison writers, but it doesn't end there. You can't cut a check and say, I've done my part. That's like putting two quarters in a homeless man's cup and call that a commitment to fighting homelessness. If you talk about it, be about it. Ride for it and rep it.

CDI: But I'm sure with the success of *Dutch*, you could find a better situation?

KT: Financially, yes no doubt. I've had several offers to do just that, but…. I believe in what Teri is doing. I believe in her as a Black woman doing her own thing. The only place I could get a better deal is corporate publishers, major publishing houses, but I really want to see Teri on top, by her own terms. Too many Black men sell the sisters out, so I understand Teri's mistrust of me as a Black man and I'm willing to go the distance, "but if she pushes me away….."

CDI: You spoke of the mind of Kwame as opposed to the crime of Kwame, but yet you wrote *Dutch*, a crime-laden, violent book. Is this also apart of the mind of Kwame?

KT: KRS One dropped "Criminal Minded" but claimed to be a teacher. He clarified the apparent contradiction and said, "To teach the people, first you have to get their attention." I agree. Even with God, when he sends miracles, isn't this a method of getting the people's attention? I'm not saying miracles are criminal in nature, but they are violations of law, no? So I say that to put law in a better perspective. Yes, Dutch is a gangsta but because everyone loves a gangsta, I used him to get the people's attention. "*Dutch II* and *III* will establish the method to my madness. Just as gangsta, but believe me, like KRS One again, you must learn!

CDI: There's a growing trend of books being written about the streets, what are your feelings about that?

KT: I applaud it. The first step in establishing your future, establishing your identity is defining your reality as opposed to having it defined for you. The majority of Black books have been written about Blacks trying to fit in to American life, American culture. Even *Invisible Man* wasn't about invisibility outside of the context, but in relation to it. Now the criminal element is finding its voice, telling its own story and in telling it, we'll find the answers and solutions on how to improve it. I have faith in the power of creativity.

CDI: It's seems these books have peaked the interest of urban youth, is this problematic or beneficial?

KT: Anything taken to excess is, or can be, problematic. No doubt. But examine this dynamic. The youth have been desensitized by the constant flood of sex and violence. But why I ask you, is a culture of e-kids [electronic kids] programmed by technology even interested in something as sensually trivial as a book? A simple book, words. That is why I look to rough muddy water and see dry land. Something is missing and kids are hungry. That is the potential. But to the naysayers, the critics, I say do something. If "Dutch" offends you, promote Toni Morrison, reading drives, creative writing classes. If I am a villain, don't just heckle me, take the stage! I challenge you to do so. But if all you can do is frown up and look down your noise, then your inactivity compounds the problem. Like Bill Cosby and his comments on low income. Just because you sent a person to college, even 1,000 people to college, what about the other 100,000? No one can help everybody but that doesn't give anyone the right to blanket criticism. Tell Bill to pay some bills, rent, take these single mothers away from the 2 and 3 jobs they work, leaving next to no time to raise kids. Then, he can talk, until then, stick to Jell-O pops.

CDI: You have written 2 books in prison, jail hasn't stopped you. What can you pass on to people in similar situations?

KT: No matter where you are, you can be heard. No matter who you are, you can make a difference, but a closed mouth don't get fed. Remember that. The attitude of a hungry cat isn't what can I do but what can't you do? And never think you have nothing to lose because you always have something to lose; a better opportunity. Utilize your resources and lastly, holla at me! P.O. Box 201, Dutley NC 28333. Whatever I can do, it's done, God willing. But you have to take the initiative.

CDI: What can we expect in the future?

KT: Initiative. I hope this article will spark interest in those who read it to reach out to me. Not only can you help me, but maybe I can help you. Maybe not today maybe not tomorrow but soon and when you need it most. But concretely, I want to establish a monopoly on ghetto distribution. Clothes, CDs, DVDs, spoons, cups, anything that comes through the ghetto and it isn't hard because the solution is on every corner and we call it "Operation: How to Rob the Industry". Oh yeah, cop my books! Your boy needs bail money!!! We're also doing *Dutch* as an independent film. Forget Hollywood, we're hitting the streets for the illest sounds and freshest faces. C-Murder is executive producer of the soundtrack.

Anyone interested send demo CD to:
141 Robert E. Lee Blvd. #154
New Orleans, LA 70124
And your bio/pictures
(to be in the movie):
Dutch Film
P.O. Box 1263 Wilmington, NC 28402
www.thelostrenaissance.com

The Republicans secret weapon for the 2008 Presidential Elections "Reaganstein!"

THE DISCO FEVER

BY IVETTE "THE DIVA" VALENTIN

A SHORT HISTORY LESSON IN HIP-HOP WITH SAL ABATIELLO

Sal Abatiello is a club promoter, club owner, record producer, business entrepreneur, actor, record label owner and one of the most memorable names in hip-hop and freestyle music. He has been on television, in *People* magazine and has given millions of dollars to the United Negro College Fund. He was the man who gave Run DMC, The Fat Boys, Kurtis Blow, Doug E. Fresh and a few other legends the opportunity to display their talents. A historical hip-hop movie called "Krush Groove" was about the beginning of hip-hop and how Sal's club, The Disco Fever, displayed the talents of many hip-hop legends. If you remember the young Italian guy with all the gold chains and the open shirts then you remember Sal. Sal thanks Russell Simmons for giving him the publicity and is proud of Russell and says that from the beginning, Russell knew how to infiltrate the system. Sal still owns Fever Records and is still in the entertainment business. The artists Sal helped put in the spotlight such as LL Cool J and Run DMC, have all moved on and made history, but Sal remains loyal to his native Bronx and is still circulating the club circuit. I had the opportunity to speak to him about his role in hip-hop. Here is his story on how it all started.

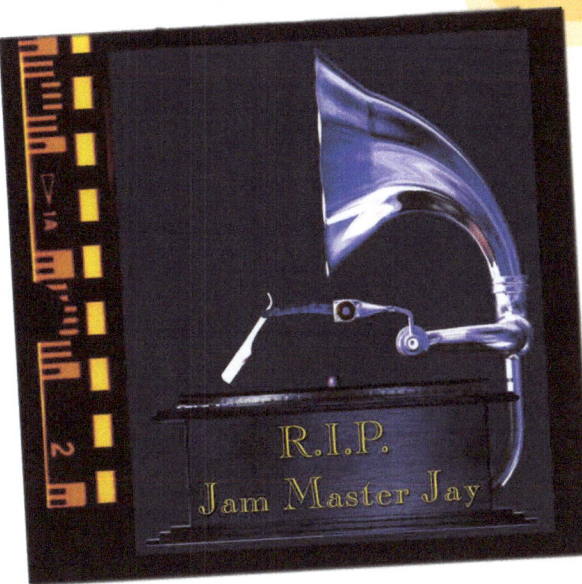

Sal, you have been in the business since 1976, correct?

Sal-
Actually 1970, 1970 was the first time I worked in a nightclub, my father owned the club. I was 17 years old, I just finished high school, and my dad was in the bar business all his life. By the time I was 18 years old, I was behind the bar not knowing anything and within a year or two, I ended up becoming one of the best bartenders in the Bronx. This was during all the Mafia days in the Bronx with all the Italian places. In my place, Chazz Palmieri was in the band along with Joe Pesci. They were just guys in the band before they were stars. They played a lot in the club I worked in and the bandstand was behind the bar. So it was me and the band behind the bar. I remained a bartender from 1970 to 1973. For some reason, I rented out "Marina Del Rey" in the Bronx, the place by Tremont near the water. I hired a group called the Tramps, who sang, "Disco Inferno." I did my first show there when I was 19 years old and was able to sell 450 tickets all on my own. On my own, when there were no cell phones, no e-mails, no radio. It was just paper flyers. I got my first taste of the promotion business and I don't know why I did it. I started noticing I had the knack to draw people. I was good at knowing what would be a hit or not and then I started out checking big discos. I heard about DJs and no one in the Bronx had DJs, only the discos like Studio 54. I turned one of my father's failing restaurants into a club and called it The Playhouse and we were the first club with a DJ. My father had talked about opening up a disco in the Bronx for an older crowd. We were trying to come up with a name and my mom came up with the name, *Disco Fever*. At that time the movie *Saturday Night Fever* was being shown at theaters. At first we didn't like the name, but we eventually thought it was hot. The club drew an older crowd and I tried to do promotions on Sundays and it wasn't working because no one believed the bands would perform live. Then one night we had a DJ by the name of *Sweet G* take over for the regular DJ. Sweet G only took over for the last hour. He would start off by doing nursery rhymes over the music and as I am watching the crowd, he is saying, "Throw your hands in the air and say HO!" and the crowd is responding back and forth. This is around 1976 and I have never seen anything like this. DJs like *Wolfman Jack* used to talk over the music before but during the disco era, no one ever talked over the music. I found the talking to be really good because it would allow the people at the bar who were not dancing to get involved. That took care of a lot of the single people back then. For it looked like a nice way in meeting people because they were all doing the same thing. So I started asking around about other DJs like *Grandmaster Flash*. Sweet G wasn't really a professional dj, but he told me about all these other guys. Sweet G was an older guy that worked a regular job during the day. I was about 25 then when I was at the Fever. So here I am going around inquiring about hip-hop and I meet Grandmaster Flash in the park. He was very young and the crowd was older. I didn't even think he was right for the club because he was really "street-looking." I started going out to this club called "371", also located on 167th Street and who was there? *DJ Hollywood* and a Spanish guy named *DJ Junebug* (who turned out to be one of the greatest DJs of all time). So now I'm watching Hollywood, who was the perfect DJ for the older crowd. He wore a suit jacket and he had routines in which the whole crowd would respond back and forth. Meanwhile, I'm trying to talk Junebug into coming out to the club but no one then wanted to come to the Fever because it was still an older, mature crowd. I now wanted to break into this hip-hop thing. I said to myself, "I know this shit is to do shit."

What made you decide to take the plunge from targeting an over 35 crowd to a younger generation?

Sal-
I wasn't trying to change the club; I stumbled on to something that was going to be groundbreaking. I liked that the crowd that wasn't dancing was being involved and as a bar owner that was the hardest part. This would bring the whole club together as one. I ended up going back to Flash and I saying, "Look, I have a spot and i'm going to make you famous if you'll come and play at this place." He asked me how? I replied, "You're going to have a steady place every night and get yourself off of the street corner. I'm going to put you in a spot where many people are going to see you, a place where maybe you can get a break." Now Flash was already a star back then, even though there were no records. He would probably make between $500 to $1000 a night but he was only working once every two months. I told him I would give him $50 a week. I also told him it wasn't about the money but about having a spot in a real disco. A place where people can come to see you and take you seriously and he brought the *Furious Five* with him. It was just me, Sweet G, Flash and a barmaid working and before you knew it the place was going crazy. I asked myself, "Holy shit, what did we just stumble on?" We later ended up getting security, expanding the club, and that was the beginning of the story.

I started getting a different rapper every night and every popular Hip-Hop rapper there in my club every night of the week.

From the time you opened up the Fever to now, what differences do you see in the industry now when it comes to the music and the atmosphere?

Sal- Back then the 18-year-olds were dancing with the 40-year-olds. I was lucky, I stumbled on music that's going to be around for hundreds of years and I stumbled on the forefront of it and I helped bring it indoors center stage. We were at the birth of it, so I am one of the pioneers. In the beginning it was party music, back then there were no crews, a crew was seven people. There was violence in the street, but it was something we would handle ourselves. Me, being a White person made it different for those that never really knew a White person. A lot of them didn't even know a White person to go up and talk to or hang out with. They were instructed not to, there was prejudice. White people didn't like Black people. Black people didn't like white people. It took them a long time to trust me as a person; they accepted me only in the club because white people owned most of the things in that neighborhood. What they liked about me was that I was young, I could dance, and they knew I knew music. And every day I had to prove myself to show them I was here from the Bronx. They would ask me why I was in their neighborhood and I would try to explain that it was my neighborhood. I was just one of those white people that didn't move away. My father has been on 169th and Third Avenue since 1930. I loved the Bronx. I never knew prejudice when I was little. Growing up in my house at Christmas the table was half Black or Spanish people. When I went to Catholic school when I was about 9 years old, then I found prejudice when I would hang out with the only Black kid in the school. When I had my Black friends in my pool the White neighbors would tell us to change the damn pool water and I never knew why. I was discovering music where my customers were becoming recording artists by the week. I was in some sick shit then; this was something that happened once in a hundred years, maybe once in fifty years. Every one was coming from the same radius, the same block. This was just the Bronx; they weren't coming from all over. Queens and Jersey started coming two or three years after the Fever. It was a radius of about 100 blocks. Now, Russell Simmons is a college kid, he's coming to the Fever. Now I'm playing hip-hop seven nights a week. I brought the first TV cameras into the club so the show can be seen throughout the entire club. We had gong shows and we gave away recording contracts. Orange "Juice Jones" was in the gong show, Slick Rick, Force MDs, and I am sure they were a few other recording artists that I just don't remember. Picture a 16-year-old Doug E. Fresh walking in the club and telling me how great he is and I'm like, "Yeah." He says, "Let me get up there." And I let him get up there and I said, "Oh, my God, this kid is going to be a star." Or Run DMC comes in and Russell tells me, "Can you put my brother on?" Run DMC would do their first show there. When you got to the Fever the recording artists would be hanging out with the gangster, the pimp, the killer, a doctor, a lawyer. This is what the Fever was about. When you got in the Fever it was about dancing, partying, and no problems. I taught everybody their jobs and I hired ex-cons and those out of work. Then I got community-minded. The turning point in my career was when I started that basketball league, which is still going on today 25 years later. Me, Mr. Magic and this guy called Greg from a rap group called the Disco Four. I sponsored and promoted it. Back then there was a lot of independence; you can get a record on the radio. DJs would take a chance. Now DJs are the stars. Rappers are such big artists now you can't even meet them. They can't perform in a club, you can't meet them. You don't see celebrities unless you go to some hustler club or if they are in a club they are jammed up in the VIP room or in the corner with 85 security guards and nobody ever meets anybody. When you went to the Fever, you met everybody and that's the difference. You can't meet a celebrity today, when somebody gets a hit record they don't do a club circuit they go straight to the Garden.

What do you think is the reason for that now?

Sal- They want to get paid. It got too big, it blew up too big. And they don't give a fuck they just want to get paid.

Do you think everyone is getting into rap for the money, for the love of it or for the actual music?

Sal- It's to do a hustle. All the drug dealers don't have to be drug dealers no more; they just got to start a record company. They just have to be a rapper; they just got to produce a record. Not to say they didn't have the talent they had the talent but that's their new hustle. It's about making money. Do they love it? Yeah but the bottom line is I don't care if you love your wife, you still want to make money. And if you are broke most likely you'll break up with your wife.

MUG SHOTS 21 Gunz Salute

Fred Hampton Jr.

MF Doom

RBG (Revolutionary But Gangsta)

DJ Oreon & Derek Jeter

Mos Def, M1 & Crew

MF Grimm (Day By Day Ent.)

Justifiable Homicide

Production Companies: Gabriel Films & Reality Films
Producers: Jonathan Stack & Jon Osman
Director: Jon Osman
Co-director: Jonathan Stack
Co-producers: Channel 4 UK
                Simon Nasht
                Radical Media
Camera: Jon Osman, Teymoore Nabili
Music: Wendy Blackstone
Editors: David Moore, Frank Kauredren, Jon Osman

Justifiable Homicide is a feature documentary based on the brutal murder of two young Puerto Rican men Antonio Rosario and Hilton Vega who were both shot by two NYPD detectives in the Bronx in early 1995. One of the detectives was Mayor Giuliani's former bodyguard. The story follows Margarita Rosario, as she transforms from a mourning mother and aunt to a powerful community activist, questioning the police officers' actions and raising the possibility of a cover-up.

Jon Osman
At the age of sixteen, Jon Osman moved from New York City to Los Angeles where he became interested in film. His career began as a post-production sound mixer where he participated in the production of many feature films. A few of his film credits include *Defending Your Life* (Meryle Streep), *Bill & Ted's Bogus Journey* (Keanu Reeves), *L.A. Story* (Steve Martin) *Trial by Jury* (William Hurt), *Drop Zone* (Wesley Snipes), and many others. In 1994 Jon returned to New York to study film directing at N.Y.U. During his studies, he directed several experimental fiction shorts and a documentary short entitled *Subway Tracks*, a film that explores the lives of musicians who perform in the subways of New York City. Subway Tracks achieved several awards including the I.D.A. student documentary award in 1996 and the Cine Golden Eagle Student Award in 1997. In late 1998, Jon began the production of *Justifiable Homicide*, a feature documentary about a mother who challenges the NYPD and Mayor Giuliani in the brutal murder of her son and nephew at the hands of two detectives in the Bronx. *Justifiable Homicide*' was completed in 2001 and has been seen in festivals around the world. Jon is currently preparing for his next feature film.

Contact Jon Osman - Jon@realityfilms.net

Bruce George, Co-Founder of *Def Poetry Jam*, founder of *The Bandana Republic*, former member of the 5 Percent Nation, former Kaos Crew member, former Casanova Crew member, former member of The Mighty Zulu Nation, former member and current affiliate of The Black Panther Collective, current affiliate with several O/G/ B's in NYC. You can e-mail Bruce George at bruce.george2@verizon.net.

The Bandana Republic:
An Anthology of Poetry & Prose by Gang Members & Affiliates

The Bandana Republic is an anthology of creative literature, including poetry (free verse, rap, spoken word, haiku), short stories, letters, and interviews written by individuals who are either former or are current gang members or are closely affiliated. The Bandana Republic is the brainchild of Mr. Bruce George, who was also executive producer/co-creator of *Def Poetry Jam* along with Russell Simmons. He also played a role in it reaching Broadway two years ago. This book is a new approach to the way books are being written, especially with the entire buzz about gangster novels and magazines. The Bandana Republic project turns a situation that is so often looked at as a negative and reveals the positive that is almost always overlooked by the mainstream media.

Gangs -R -Us — by Bruce George

We are societies bastard child
overlooked
gate-keeper
sanctioned
banned
and abandoned
until we make noise
flash our toys
you see we are watching
watching you clutch your bags
but our rags
has the same value as yours
and if you look at our sores
you will see blood
that has clotted
yet you rather us dearly departed
from life
over turf
and for what its worth
you are just the same
same shit
different name
like Landlords and Owners
loan Sharks and loaners
it's still a crime
and on earth
we're doing time
just like you
hate
just like you
cry
just like you
pray
just like you
war
just like you
like you
like you
are better
whether Swiss, American Cheese or Cheddar
we're chasing dreams
opposite ends of extremes
but no less than
and as long as there's oppression
we will set-trip to Heaven
for all have fallen short
we kill for rep
Y'all kill for sport
for your crimes are Federal
for our 10 kills to your million
made you a General!

COUP D'ETAT ILLUSTRATED | BOOK REVIEW | VOLUME 1

BAYOAN B. CORTES
Creative Director
& Tattoo Specialist

/ GUERRERO
Graphic Designer
& Copywriter

GORILLA CONVICT
PUBLICATIONS

NBN
No Borders, No Boundaries

No Borders, No Boundaries is the Graphic Design & Illustration studio founded in 2006 by Bayoan "Bee" Cortes and J. "Guerrero" Beltrán. Outside the box where non-conformity exists, NBN's vision combines two distinctive forms, raw imagery and creative text. Both of which create urban contemporary art that appeals to all the masses no matter where they fall on the "scale." NBN will not only reface the art and advertising medium pertaining to the mainstream Hip-Hop culture, it will revolutionize it.

WWW.MYSPACE.COM/NBNGRAPHICS

This is the publishing house where the edges of fiction and reality collide. Founded by prisoners for prisoners and the world at large, GCP gives a voice to writers emerging from the depths of America's gulags. Life in the belly of the beast can be vicious and our Gorilla Convict soldiers give it to you raw and on the edge with tales from prison, street novels and real life stories from the criminal underworld.

To order books or learn more go to

WWW.GORILLACONVICT.COM

Police Department
Intelligence Bureau Information Summary
January 2005

NAME OF SUBJECT	ALIAS	ALIAS	ALIAS
Robert Perez	Chino	Godfather	

RESIDENCE ADDRESS	HOME PHONE	SOCIAL SECURITY NO.	D.P.D. NO	F.B.I. NO.
████	████	████	████	████

BUSINESS ADDRESS	BUSINESS PHONE	OTHER	GROUP ASSOCIATION
████	████	████	La Westside Familia

DOB	RACE	SEX	HGT	WGT	HAIR	EYES	DEFORMATIES
11/22/61	Boriqua	Male	5'10	170	Black	Brown	

TATOOS AND OTHER DISTINGUISHING CHARACTERISTICS
Skulls, RIP, FTW, Che, Guns, Knives, Names, Unknown Tats

VEHICLE MAKE	YEAR	STYLE	COLOR	LIC NO.	STATE	YEAR	TYPE	DRIVER'S LIC NO	STATE

Police Department Copies of Purged Intelligence File
Released to: *Lerry Wigle*
By:
Date: 1/1/302

ASSOCIATE'S NAME	ADDRESS	ASSOCIATES'S NAME	ADDRESS
George Morillo, aka Scarface, aka Squeeze Gunz		Guillo Perez, aka Big Willie, aka Big Guillo	
Alex Sedano, aka Big Al, aka Al Sawed Off		Louis Santos, aka Louie Lou	

Way before Roc-A-Fella Records and Jay-Z began to use the words "La Familia" in their ads, the real "La Familia" was putting in work out in the streets of the upper Westside of Manhattan, since 1979 to be exact. Don't get it twisted, "La Familia" was not only gang banging in a gang-filled city of the 70s, 80s and 90s, it was also a strong community activist organization. ████ La Westside Familia, as it's also ████ known, has seen the evolution of the streets ████ and street gangs.
In the early era there were outlaw gang's like "*The Sandman*"(Manhattan), "*The Ching-A-Lings*"(Bronx), "*Crazy Homicides*"(East New York), "*The Golden Guineas*"(North Bronx),"*Homicide Incorporated*"(Coney Island), "*The Black Spades*"(Bronx), the "*Black Bitches*"(Canarsie), "*The War Pigs*"(North Bronx), the "*Mau Mau Girls*"(Flatbush), "*Power*"(Bronx), "*The Royal Charmers*" (South Bronx)', "*Savage Nomads*"(Manhattan), "*The Aliens*"(North Bronx), "*The Savage Skulls*"(Bronx), the "*Seven Crowns*"(Bronx), "*Savage Samurai's*"(Manhattan), "*The Ministers*" (Bronx), "*Seven Immortals*"(Bronx), and many others.

By 1970, gang membership rose as high as 11,000. Gangs in the 1970s ran shit in all corners of New York City and everywhere in between. By 1973 there was an estimated 315 gangs in New York City, claiming 19,503 members. And crime, to put it bluntly, was out of control. At the same time some gangs were still able to put work into the revolution of the 60s and 70s. "*The Royal Charmers*" of the South Bronx, ordered that no drug dealers or junkies would be allowed on Hoe Avenue. During the height of the heroin epidemic any who violated this order were brutally beaten or killed. Gangs like "*The Black Spades*" ████ worked on getting poor people registered to vote, and helped raise money for sickle cell ████ anemia. "La Familia" also kept drugs out of the community, and organized block clean-ups because the city refused to commit to quality of life for its poorest residents.

In the 80s gang warfare peaked as the numbers of gang and crews grew with the introduction of crack ████ cocaine to the inner city, and the explosion of the hip-hop culture. The ████ outlaw gangs evolved into new ones, like the once known "Black Spades" became the great "Zulu Nation." You began to see gangs hit the streets with a vengeance. Gangs saw big money in destroying their own communities. Drug dealings, murders, rapes and robberies where all part of the game. Shit, these gangs did play the game, including the "*Ball Busters*"(Washington Heights), the "*Decepticons*"(Brooklyn), "*Young Talented Children*"(Manhattan), the "*Wild Cowboys*"(Manhattan), "*Preachers Crew*"(Harlem), the "*Royal Play Boys*"(Manhattan), "*Young City Boys*"(Manhattan), "*Natural Born Killers*"(Manhattan), "*Gerry Curls Gang*"(Manhattan), "*Dead On Arrival*"(Manhattan).

In the mid to late 1990s "La Familia" continued to do its part in the struggle by ████ being a major part in a project called the "*United Family Coalition*." The "UFC" was a collective effort by political ████ organizations along with street organizations to come together and curb some of

R.I.P.
Cowboy
Thomas Santos
Big Joey
Nena
Louie AKA "Tiger"

R.I.P.
Big Marta
Lil Johnny
Big Ralphy
Diane

Police Department
Intelligence Bureau Information Summary
January 2005

the ills we faced in the inner city: violence, police brutality, racial injustice, crime, drugs, spousal abuse, a decaying educational system, homelessness and a racially bias legal system. The coalition had organizations like the "National Congress for Puerto Rican Rights", "Zulu Nation", the "Black Panther Collective", the ███████████████████ "Almighty Latin ███████████ Kings and Queens Nation", the "Netas", "Aliaza Dominicana", and several "Bloods" chapters. Eventually, the effort was stopped by outside forces.

In the late 60s and early 70s, Chino worked with the "Young Lords Party" and that is where La Familia got its political consciousness. "La Familia" may have started out as kids aged twelve to fifteen, but together they assumed power far beyond their age. That power struck fear and respect in the hearts of any and everybody in the neighborhood, as well as those coming from other neighborhoods. Together, they were invincible. You couldn't fuck with one member of "La Familia" without fucking with them all. This loyalty, unity and commitment were and still are the mentality of the few that are still around from that crazy era in NYC history. Like Chino a living icon of the streets with his many untold stories, where pain and joy are sometimes the same thing. We are proud to introduce you to THE LAST OF A DYING BREED: Robert "Chino" Perez.

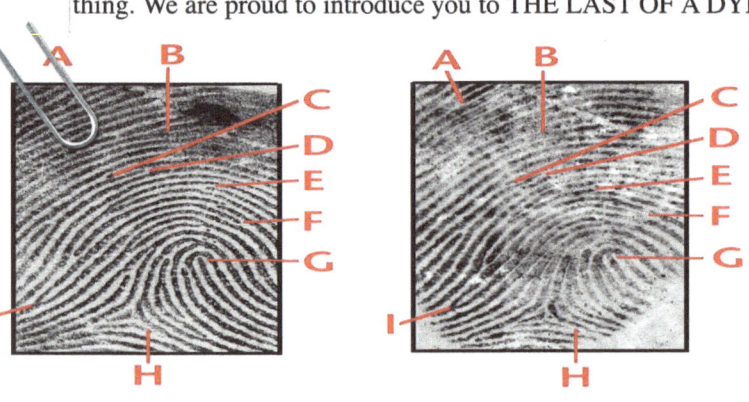

Ron Kuby and Chino

Coup D'Etat Illustrated: At what age were you introduced to the streets?
Robert "Chino" Perez: At the age of 10 or 11 years old, that's when I started hanging in the streets and I got myself, not influenced but involved with people that were in gangs . That's how I got started and continued. I started hanging out and being involved in gangs and people that were older then me and I took advice from a lot of them. I grew up just being a leader, not a follower because I was always a leader, I never followed nobody. But I really was influenced by the older people who gave me advice on everything. I took their advice and then later, I began giving people advice.

Coup D'Etat Illustrated: What was it like growing up in New York City in your era?
Robert "Chino" Perez: At that time it was much different than what it is now. People were really united and together. Neighborhoods were more organized. But, after the years went things changed. The rents increased, and people left the neighborhood. In my time there had been real togetherness.

Coup D'Etat Illustrated: When did you get involved in politics, and why?
Robert "Chino" Perez: I got involved in politics when I was 11 years old. I was taken to a demonstration and after that I started going to demonstrations. I started organizing my own block clean-ups in my neighborhood. And why did I get involved in that? Because the people that guided me to the right path they gave me the advice which helped me to change my life to where it is right now.

Coup D'Etat Illustrated: What gangs or crews were you running with before "La Familia"?
Robert "Chino" Perez: I first started hanging out, with the "*Hynch-Man Nomads*" at 109th Street. Then I started with "The Savage Skulls" in the Bronx, and "Savage Nomads," and "The Sand-Mans." Then I went to Brooklyn and ended up with "La Familia." That experience then helped me bring it to the Westside and start La Westside Familia.

Police Department
Intelligence Bureau Information Summary
January 2005

Coup D'Etat Illustrated: What are outlaw gangs?
Robert "Chino" Perez: An outlaw gang is when you are committed to a gang family and you are dedicated to that family, in dress, boots, chains, and your jacket patches. An outlaw gang, one thing is certain is that when it comes down, when the whole family has to come down or whatever it is, you are there and you are going to participate and you are going to put your life down with your family. Outlaw is when you're dedicated to your family that's not your immediate family; it's your family from the streets.

Coup D'Etat Illustrated: When did you start "La Familia", and why did you feel a need to start up a gang?
Robert "Chino" Perez: Familia really came out in 1979, we all grew up together, and had been together for many years before that. But 1979 we all became La Westside Familia. We didn't need to start it, we already had it, we just gave it the name.

Coup D'Etat Illustrated: What does the name mean?
Robert "Chino" Perez: The name means a family. To me a family that I could always count on. That I can call when I need advice a little push to get going. A family that will never pull me backwards.

Coup D'Etat Illustrated: What is "La Familia's" memberships race and/or nationality?
Robert "Chino" Perez: We had everyone. We had Italians, (Big Joey RIP), we had Dominicans, Puerto Ricans, Colombians, Blacks, Mexicans, Cubans, Ecuadorians, Shit, we have every nationality, because we are not into being prejudice, we're a family.

Coup D'Etat Illustrated: Where, was "La Familia" neighborhood base?
Robert "Chino" Perez: 93rd Street and Columbus Ave. in Manhattan was our base, but we had all the 90s, and some of the 80s from Central Park to Riverside Drive.

Coup D'Etat Illustrated: What have been your highs and lows after all these years?
Robert "Chino" Perez: The greatest feeling was when I graduated from high school and I gave my mother the satisfaction to see me graduate from school. And my low was when I was in a cell; I had to listen while they told me what to do and what not to do.

Coup D'Etat Illustrated: What do you see in the future for street gangs here in NYC?
Robert "Chino" Perez: Right now the government is trying to destroy everything, there's not going to be street gangs in the future. If the gangs don't get together and organize, and get involved in politics, and with the people in the community there will be no future for gangs.

Coup D'Etat Illustrated: How would you like "Chino" and "La Familia" to be remembered?
Robert "Chino" Perez: I would like to be remembered those young kids who look up and say, well I always had someone from La Familia. Not just me, but any of my people, to say they always gave me advice, they kept me out of trouble and they always looked out for me. I didn't get beat up or whatever. I always had somebody I could run to, and they helped me.

Coup D'Etat Illustrated: Chino, is there anything else you might want to add?
Robert "Chino" Perez: I would like the world to know that I will always be me. I will never change no matter what the fuck comes through. No matter what goes up and what comes down, I will always be me. Chino Familia, FTW, death before dishonor.

We're outlaws because when the constitution and the laws of this country were written we were not included, and we are still denied involvement in that process till this day. So until that changes, we'll keep our guns close and continue to live like outlaws till we die. -Squeeze

FAMILIES AGAINST MANDATORY MINIMUMS FOR REAL LIFE

By: Seth "Soul Man" Ferranti
www.gorillaconvict.com

Last October, the 20th anniversary of federal mandatory minimum sentencing guidelines passed with no fanfare. The 1986 Anti-Drug Abuse Act – spurred on in Congress by basketball star Len Bias's drug related death and the crack wars that made Washington DC the murder capital of the world – was signed into law by President Ronald Reagan. Since then, taxpayers have spent billions of dollars annually fighting our government's "War on Drugs," which has directly resulted in filling prisons with low-level drug offenders and first-time, non-violent felons.

Mandatory sentencing laws have forced judges to give fixed prison terms to those convicted of specific crimes, most often drug offenses. These laws have disproportionately affected people of color with a 100 to 1 crack-cocaine ratio. Because of their severity, families have been destroyed in the name of justice. Throughout the years, there have been many critics of the "War on Drugs" and the mandatory minimum sentences, but the leading advocate for reform has been Families Against Mandatory Minimums (FAMM). The mission of this national, non-profit organization – founded in 1991 – is to challenge the inflexible and excessive penalties required by mandatory minimum sentencing laws.

"We celebrated our 15th year anniversary in October," says Lani Poblete, FAMM's Communications Director. "Julie Stewert is the president and founder of FAMM. She formed the organization when her brother, a non-violent, first-time drug offender was sentenced to five years in federal prison for growing marijuana. Julie had never heard of mandatory sentencing laws and she was outraged that the judge no longer had the discretion to make the punishment fit the crime. Julie started FAMM to promote fairer sentencing laws."

Since its inception, FAMM has directly contributed to fairer sentences for over 45,000 drug defendants nationwide and paved the way for the current shift away from mandatory sentencing policies. With 36,000 members, a quarterly newsletter, The FammGram, and website FAMM.org, the organization works to end mandatory sentencing laws by educating the public, lobbying federal and state lawmakers, building coalitions, and promoting grassroots efforts. Their newsletter and widely-visited website provide comprehensive coverage of federal sentencing policies, legal news, prison news and media reports, and serves as a resource for media, students and the general public.

"We have wanted to think of more ways to promote FAMM to a broader audience," Lani says of the little organization that is making big noise in our nation's capital. "Only eight people, including Julie, work in the DC office. Then we have staff that work in various satellite offices around the country."

It isn't easy, but with righteousness on their side, FAMM has accomplished a lot. But taking on the federal government, mandatory minimums, and the 100 to 1 crack-cocaine ratio disparity isn't easy. FAMM needs more members.

To learn more please visit: www.FAMM.org

www.ingramcontent.com/pod-product-compliance
Lightning Source LLC
Chambersburg PA
CBHW061030180426
43192CB00034B/74